EXTENDING

Word 97

for Windows

CAROL MCKENZIE & PAT BRYDEN

Heinemann Educational Publishers,
Halley Court, Jordan Hill, Oxford OX2 8EJ
a division of Reed Educational & Professional Publishing Ltd

Heinemann is a registered trademark of Reed Educational
& Professional Publishing Limited

OXFORD FLORENCE PRAGUE MADRID ATHENS
MELBOURNE AUCKLAND KUALA LUMPUR SINGAPORE TOKYO
IBADAN NAIROBI KAMPALA JOHANNESBURG GABORONE
PORTSMOUTH NH (USA) CHICAGO MEXICO CITY SAO PAULO

First published 1998
2002 2001 2000 99
10 9 8 7 6 5 4 3 2 1

A catalogue record for this book is available from the British Library on request.

ISBN 0 435 45430 7

Designed by Moondisks

Typeset by TechType, Abingdon, Oxon

Printed and bound in Great Britain by The Bath Press, Bath

Screen shots reprinted with permission from Microsoft Corporation

▶ Contents

▶ RSA Text Processing Schemes

RSA Examinations Board has designed a suite of Text Processing schemes at Stages I, II and III. The overall aim of these modular awards is to meet the business document production requirements of the discerning employer and to give candidates the opportunity to demonstrate competence in text processing skills to the level demanded for NVQ Administration.

Stage I indicates that the candidate has sufficient knowledge or skill to begin employment, although further study would be beneficial.

Stage II shows a sound understanding of and competence in the subject and a recommendation for employment. It also suggests that someone who holds such a certificate may well benefit from advanced studies.

Stage III indicates an all-round knowledge and understanding of the subject and, in the practical skills, a very high degree of proficiency.

At each stage, there is a *Part 1* examination which assesses candidates' ability to produce a variety of routine business documents. A selection of *Part 2* examinations assesses skills in more specific applications such as word processing, typewriting and audio-transcription.

There is a Text Processing Diploma at Stages II and III; this has been designed to recognise all-round achievement in Text Processing. The following modules which contribute to the Stage II Diploma are covered in this book:

▶ Text Processing Stage II Part 1

▶ Word Processing Stage II Part 2

▶ Mailmerge Stage II Part 2

The Diploma is awarded to candidates who demonstrate competence in the *Part 1* examination and in three *Part 2* examinations at the same stage. Additional modules include specialist applications of text processing, for example:

▶ in a foreign language

▶ using specialist terminology

▶ typewriting

▶ shorthand transcription, and

▶ audio-transcription.

▶ About this book

This book has been written as a continuation text to *Introducing Word 97 for Windows* by the same authors. It has been designed as a progressive course and is suitable for use in the classroom, in an open-learning workshop or as a private study aid.

This book has been produced to assist people who wish to gain intermediate level accreditation through the RSA Examination Board's Text Processing Schemes, using Microsoft Word 97 for Windows software package. It is anticipated that users will be familiar with the QWERTY keyboard and have basic competence in using computer hardware.

Units 1-5 are designed for students preparing to take intermediate examinations such as RSA Stage II Part 1 Text Processing. These units are also suitable for the revision of text processing skills without taking an examination.

Units 6-11 are designed for students preparing to take intermediate examinations such as RSA Stage II Part 2 Word Processing. These units are also suitable for beginners who wish to learn how to prepare multi-page documents, tables and letters from standard phrases without taking an examination.

Units 12-15 are designed for students preparing to take the RSA Stage II Part 2 Mailmerge examination. These units are also suitable for students who wish to extend their knowledge and skills to include preparation and merging of a database and standard letter without taking an examination.

A brief outline of the examination and examination practice for each stage of learning is included in Units 5, 11, and 15.

Format of the book

Printout checks for all exercises are given at the back of the book (pp. 154–194). These should be used for checking by both students and teachers/trainers.

The Progress Review Checklist (pp. 152–153) allows students to keep a record of their progress through the exercises and to note the number of errors made. If completed at the end of each working session, this checklist can be referred to quickly in order to locate the unit to be worked on next.

Command boxes for Word 97 functions are given when appropriate. Instruction is given on how to carry out the required function. The commands explain keyboard, mouse and menu operation.

The Glossary of Commands at the back of the book provides a comprehensive, alphabetically-listed quick reference for all the Word 97 commands introduced in the book. The commands are shown for keyboard, mouse and menu users. Shortcut keys are included and students may prefer to use these methods as they become more familiar with the program.

All exercise material is to be completed in Times New Roman point size 12 unless otherwise indicated.

Working through a unit

1   When you see this symbol, read all the information before you begin. You may also need to refer back to this information as you carry out the exercises.

2   When you see this symbol, carry out the exercises, following the numbered steps, eg 1.1, 1.2.

3   Use Word's spelling and grammar tool to check your document. Proofread the document carefully yourself – the spelling tool does not find every error.

4   Use the Print Preview facility to check that your document is going to be correct when printed. If it is, save your work on to your floppy disk (usually in A Drive) or into an appropriate directory. Then print your work.

5   Compare your document with the printout checks at the back of the book (pp. 154–194). (If you are using this book in class, your tutor may also wish to check your work). Correct any errors which you find in your work. Print the documents again if required to do so by your tutor. (If you are working on your own, you may not consider this necessary)

6   Complete your Progress Review Checklist. Then exit from Word 97 or begin work on the next unit (as appropriate).

Do not delete files from your disk – you may need them later!

▶ Introduction to Word 97 for Windows

Microsoft Windows is a graphical user interface, which allows the user to communicate with the computer. The graphical nature of the messages on screen makes Windows a user-friendly operating system. Microsoft Word 97 is a software package used for text processing which operates within the Windows environment.

The **mouse** is used to move a pointer to any required location on screen. The mouse has two buttons: *left* and *right*. As you move the mouse across the desk, an electronic sensor picks up the movement of the ball and moves the **mouse pointer** across the screen in the same direction.

▶ You use the mouse to *point* to the item you want on screen.

▶ You then *click* the mouse button (usually the left one) to highlight or *select* an option on screen (quickly pressing and releasing the button).

▶ Sometimes you *double-click* a mouse button (quickly pressing and releasing the button twice).

▶ You may also use a *dragging* action by holding down the mouse button, moving the mouse, and then releasing the button.

▶ If you are not sure of the function of an icon on one of the tool bars, just point to it with the mouse and wait for a second – a tool tip (Figure 1) describing the function of the icon will appear to help you.

Figure 1 Tool tip

When you start the Word 97 program, the **Document Window** in Figure 2 will be displayed on screen.

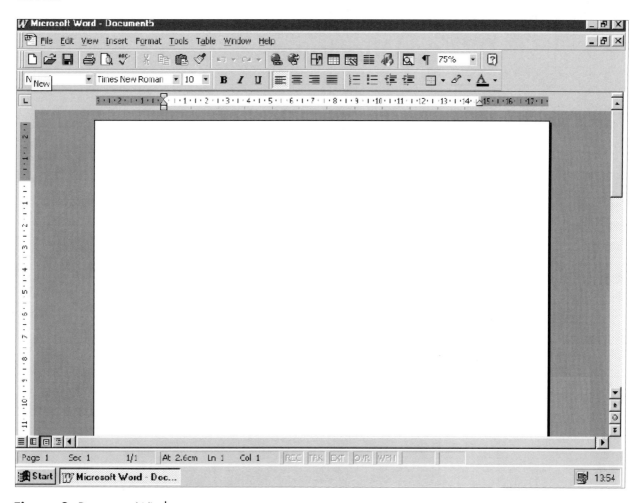

Figure 2 Document Window

The blue bar across the top of the screen is the **Title Bar**, showing the name of the application being used and the current document name.

The **Menu Bar**, shown in Figure 3, gives a list of **menu names** describing commands which can be selected by using the mouse or the keyboard.

File   Edit   View   Insert   Format   Tools   Table   Window   Help

Figure 3 Menu Bar

A **drop-down menu** then gives a further range of options within the **menu** (in Figure 4, the **View** button has been selected).

As you will see, some of the menu choices have one character underlined (eg **Ruler**). Selection can be carried out using the keyboard, eg pressing **R** in the example in Figure 4 would remove the Ruler line from the screen. The Ruler returns if you press **R** again – this is a 'toggle' switch. (A tick against a menu choice indicates that the option is currently in operation. When the tick is removed, the facility is 'switched off'.)

Selection can also be made by using the mouse. Clicking the left mouse button on **Ruler** in the above example would remove the ruler line from the screen.

Some menu choices are followed by a **keyboard shortcut**, eg

Figure 4 Drop-down menu

<u>F</u>ind...   **Ctrl + F**
<u>R</u>eplace...   **Ctrl + H**
<u>G</u>o To...   **Ctrl + G**

Holding down the **Ctrl** key and then pressing the letter shown will activate the command.

An **ellipsis** (3 dots ...) after a menu choice (eg **<u>Z</u>oom...**) indicates that you will be asked to give more information before the command can be executed.

When Word 97 needs to give or receive more information – a **dialogue box** is displayed on screen. You can move through the dialogue box using the **Tab** key or you can move the mouse pointer to the box required and click the left button. Word 97 asks you to respond by presenting information, options or questions in different ways by using boxes and buttons. The dialogue box in Figure 5 shows the different types of boxes and buttons you will meet.

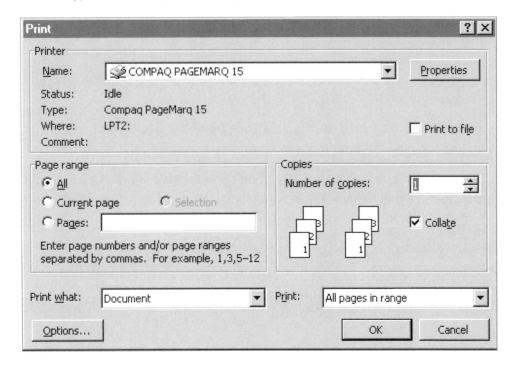

Figure 5 Dialogue Box

Clicking on [OK] confirms the information in the boxes. You can close a dialogue box without giving a command by clicking on [Cancel] or on the [x] icon at the top right of the dialogue box.

You can minimise a document window by clicking on the [_] icon. This reduces the window to a small bar at the bottom of the window.

To restore the window to its full size, click on the [⊡] icon.

When Word 97 is carrying out a function, it may ask you to wait by displaying the [⧗] hourglass icon. Wait until the hourglass has disappeared from the screen before proceeding with the next step.

The **Standard Tool Bar** (see Figure 6) is displayed on screen whilst you are working on a Word document.

Figure 6 Standard Tool Bar

This consists of a range of icons, each representing a different function related to creating and editing documents. You select a function by pointing to the icon with the mouse pointer and clicking the left mouse button. For example, clicking on the [🖶] Print icon would activate the printer to print a copy of the current document.

The use of these icons is explained more fully throughout the book.

The **Formatting Tool Bar** is also displayed on screen in a Word 97 document.

Figure 7 Formatting Tool Bar

This consists of a range of icons, each representing a different formatting option. You select a function by clicking on the icon.

The function activated by each icon is shown as a **Tool Tip**, which appears when the mouse pointer is positioned on the icon (see the **Spelling and Grammar** icon tool tip in Figure 1 on p. 1).

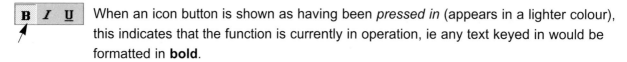 When an icon button is shown as having been *pressed in* (appears in a lighter colour), this indicates that the function is currently in operation, ie any text keyed in would be formatted in **bold**.

The **Status Bar** at the bottom of the screen displays information about the document on screen: eg the page number, section number, line number, column number etc (see Figure 8).

Figure 8 Status Bar

The current time is displayed in the bottom right hand corner of the screen (see Figure 11).

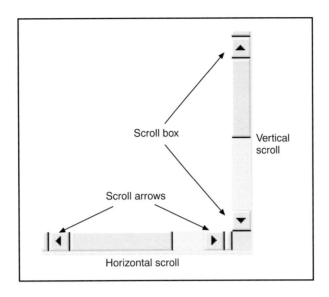

Figure 9 Scroll bars

The **Scroll Bars** at the right side and bottom of the screen allow text to be scrolled by using the mouse.

For example, clicking on the [▼] down arrow on the vertical scroll bar will move the 'document frame' downwards so that the text moves up the screen.

The horizontal Scroll Bar also displays buttons to select the different ways in which a document can be viewed (see Figure 10).

[≡|□|▣|☲]

Figure 10 Scroll Bar buttons

The **Task Bar** at the very bottom of the screen allows you to switch between applications or tasks.

Figure 11 Task Bar

Help and the Office Assistant

Word 97 offers online **Help** to users. The help command can be activated from the document screen in three ways.

▶ By selecting **Help** from the Menu Bar and then clicking on the [?] **Microsoft Word Help** icon.

▶ By clicking on the [?] **Microsoft Word Help** icon on the Standard Tool Bar.

▶ By pressing **F1** function key on the keyboard.

Activating Help in any of the previous ways brings an animated character (your Office Assistant) (see Figure 12) onto your screen, followed by a yellow text box asking 'What would you like to do?' (see Figure 13).

Figure 12 Office Assistant

You can type in a question in your own words and then click **Search**. Office Assistant will then show you a list of topics related to your question or to the task in hand. Clicking on the appropriate blue button will give you the information you require.

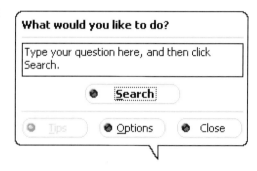

Figure 13 What would you like to do?

You may also click **Tips** to see screen tips. An example of a screen tip is shown in Figure 14.

Note: Office Assistant can change its appearance – from 'The Genius' to 'Power Pup' and from 'Shakespeare' to 'The Dot' to name but a few! If you would rather not see these delightful characters on your screen, you can 'switch them off' by:

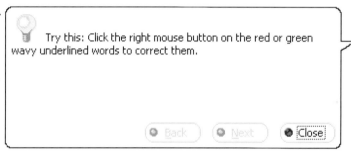

Figure 14 Screen tip

▶ clicking on the **Close** button on the Assistant's box
▶ clicking the right button anywhere in the Assistant's box and selecting **Hide Assistant**; *or*
▶ clicking the right button anywhere in the Assistant's box and selecting **Options** then clearing the **Respond to F1** key box.

Clicking the 📓 **Contents and Index** icon on the Help drop-down menu (see Figure 15) allows you to:

▶ open a 'book' containing information on Word 97 functions (Contents); *or*
▶ key in the topic on which you need help (Index).

Clicking the ⓀⓀ **What's This?** icon on the Help drop-down menu (see Figure 15) changes the mouse pointer into a question mark so that you can click on a particular item and learn about it.

Figure 15 Help drop-down menu

▶ Basic document layout and appearance

By the end of Unit 1, you will have revised how to:

▶ proofread text with the aid of the AutoCorrect and Spelling and Grammar tools
▶ format/emphasise text
▶ set the margin alignment and document line spacing
▶ indent text at left and right margins
▶ change the left and right margins and typing line length of a document

 Proofreading text ▶

Typescript containing typographical errors

In the Stage II examinations, you will be expected to carry out more complex proofreading, text editing and formatting. Text editing may involve correcting mistakes made in previous printouts. Watch out for uncorrected spelling errors and transposition errors. In the RSA examination, errors in the draft will be circled for you to correct. At work, however, it is often up to you to proofread for typographical errors, to decide what is wrong and to key in the text correctly. For example:

This sentence contians 2 transpositoin errors.

should be keyed in as:

This sentence contains 2 transposition errors.

Typescript containing spelling errors

Remember, Word 97 can help you with spelling because it has a built-in spelling and grammar check tool which checks for spelling and grammar errors as you type. Word 97 will identify a spelling error with a red wavy line and a grammatical error with a green wavy line. However, it is important to proofread the text yourself as well, as Word 97 is often unable to check proper names (eg cities, surnames etc). Also, if you have keyed in the wrong version of a word, eg *their* instead of *there*, the spellchecker will not detect this as both versions are spelt correctly. In the Stage II examination you will be expected to be able to spell a list of additional words – the errors in the draft will be circled for you. For example:

This sentance contains 3 speling errers.

should be keyed in as:

This sentence contains 3 spelling errors.

Only you can tell if you have copied names of people or places correctly and if a piece of information you were asked to find is correct. You can choose to act only on those words you want to change – if Word queries a word which you know to be correct, you can ignore the prompt to change it. If you were going to use an unusual word fairly frequently, you have an option to **Add** it to the Spellchecker memory. Spellchecker would never stop on that word again.

You will be expected to be able to spell correctly the following words, and their derivations where marked * (eg plurals, -ed, -ing, -ment, -tion, -ly, -able, -ible):

access*	believe*	discuss*	receive*
accommodate*	business*	expense*	recommend*
achieve*	client*	experience*	responsible*
acknowledge*	colleague*	financial*	separate*
advertisement*	committee*	foreign	sufficient*
although	correspondence	government*	temporary*
apparent*	definite*	inconvenient*	through
appreciate*	develop*	receipt*	

 ## Exercise 1A

1.1   Spend a little time making sure you know how to spell all the words listed above correctly – ask someone to test you!

 ## Spelling and grammar check – quick method

Click: The right mouse button on top of the word with a green or red wavy line underneath it
Click: The correction you want from the list offered

Spelling and Grammar Tool – to turn on/off

You can choose to check spelling and grammar automatically as you type. However, if you find the wavy lines distracting, you can turn this facility off temporarily and then check the entire document at once after typing.

▶   Select: **Tools**, **Options** from the menu
▶   Click: The **Spelling & Grammar** tab

To turn the facilities on:

▶   Click: **Check spelling as you type**
▶   Click: **Check grammar as you type**

To turn the facilities off:

▶   Click: **Hide spelling errors in this document**
▶   Click: **Hide grammatical errors in this document**

Spelling and grammar check – dialogue box method ▶

Keyboard	Mouse
Position the cursor: At the start of the file Press: **F7**	Position the cursor: At the start of the file Select: **Tools**, **Spelling & Grammar** from the menu
	OR
	Click: The **Spelling and Grammar** button

The **Spelling and Grammar** dialogue box is displayed on screen.

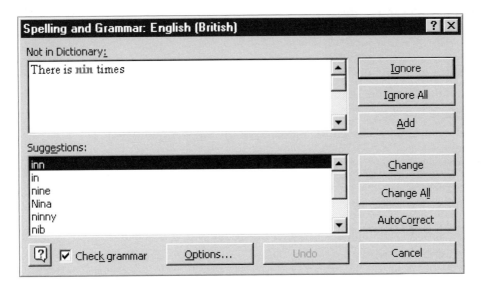

Figure 1.1 Spelling and Grammar dialogue box

▶ Word 97 tells you the error in the dialogue box and tells you what type of error it is.

▶ Word 97 highlights the most obvious replacement in the **Suggestions** box and often gives a list of other likely alternatives for you to select from.

▶ You can also edit the text yourself in the dialogue box if this is more appropriate.

Select from the spelling dialogue buttons as appropriate:

Button	Action
Ignore	Leaves the word unchanged the first time it occurs but stops on it whenever it occurs again (if you continue editing, the word **Ignore** changes to **Resume**).
Ignore All	Leaves the word unchanged on every occurrence (until you restart Word).
Change	Accepts the spelling in the dialogue box or the **Suggestions** box.
Change All	Changes the first and all subsequent occurrences of the misspelt word.
Add	Adds the word to the Dictionary.
AutoCorrect	Adds the misspelt word and its correction to the AutoCorrect list – ie, if you ever misspell this word in the same way again as you are typing, Word will correct it automatically for you!

Press: **Esc** to finish	Select: **Cancel** to finish

Note: If you do not wish to check the spelling of the whole document, you can first select/highlight a portion of text or even one word before running spellchecker.

Autocorrect – automatic correction of common keying errors

As you type, you may already have noticed that Word 97 automatically corrects some commonly misspelt words. For example, if you type 'teh' instead of 'the' or 'adn' instead of 'and' or 'i' instead of 'I', Word 97 will put it right for you. If there is a word that you often mistype or misspell, you can add it to Word's list of automatic corrections.

Autocorrect

▶ Select: **Tools**, **AutoCorrect** from the menu
▶ Check: That the **Replace Text As You Type** check box is ticked
▶ In the **Replace** box, key in: The word that you often mistype/misspell, eg unusaul
▶ In the **With** box, key in: The correct spelling of the word, eg unusual
▶ Click: **Add**
▶ Click: **OK**

Word will also make the following corrections automatically.

▶ Change the second capital letter to a lowercase letter if you accidentally type two capital letters at the beginning of a word.
▶ Capitalise the first letter at the beginning of a sentence.
▶ Capitalise the first letter of the days of the week.
▶ Reverse accidental usage of the CAPS LOCK key.

Exercise 1B

1.2 Switch on and load Word 97. Insert your work disk in to the disk drive (unless you are saving documents on the hard drive or network).

1.3 A good use of AutoCorrect is for replacing shortened versions of words which you find particularly difficult to spell – when you key in the shortened version, Word 97 will automatically replace it with the correct spelling for you. Select **AutoCorrect** from the **Tool** menu. Enter the replacements (**Replace:**) of common misspellings and the correctly spelt versions (**With:**) shown below:

Replace:	With:
acc	accommodate
advert	advertisement
rec	receive
sep	separate

1.4 To test your AutoCorrect entries, with a clear screen, key in the following, pressing the Tab key between each word:

acc　　　　　**advert**　　　　　　**rec**　　　　　**sep**

If you have followed the instructions for AutoCorrect correctly, Word should automatically have converted your entries to appear on the screen as:

Accommodate　　　**advertisement**　　　**receive**　　　**separate**

Note: AutoCorrect will only insert replacement entries exactly as they were entered. You would not, for instance, be able to automatically substitute the word 'accommodation' instead of 'accommodate'. Although 'rec' could also be the abbreviation for 'receipt', Word would automatically reproduce it as 'receive'. You would either have to key in the whole word correctly, or edit the AutoCorrect entry as appropriate.

1.5 Close the file without saving, ready for the next exercise.

Document appearance and layout ▶

You will also be expected to carry out more complex text-formatting procedures at Stage II. This may include emphasising the text, changing the alignment of the left margin, and/or changing the line spacing. These topics were dealt with in the first book of this series, but a summary is included here for easy reference.

Formatting/emphasising text ▶

Format/Emphasis	Keyboard	Mouse
Bold	Press: **Ctrl + B**	Click: The **B** Bold button
Italics	Press: **Ctrl + I**	Click: The *I* *I*talics button
Underline	Press: **Ctrl + U**	Click: The **U** <u>U</u>nderline button
Change font	Press: **Ctrl + Shift + F**	Click: The **Font** button
	Select: A font from the list	Select: A font from the list
Change font size	Press: **Ctrl + Shift + P**	Click: The **Font Size** button
Next larger point size:	Press: **Ctrl +]**	Select: A point size from the list
Next smaller point size:	Press: **Ctrl + [**	
Remove emphasis	Select: Text to change back	Select: Text to change back
(back to plain text)	Press: **Ctrl + Spacebar**	Click: The appropriate button
Highlight text		Click: The 🖉 **Highlight** button

To format text while typing:
▶ Click: The appropriate command button (eg to switch bold text on, click on the **B** button)
▶ Key in: The text
▶ Click: The appropriate command button again to switch the emphasis off

To format existing text:

▶ Select: The text to be changed

▶ Click: The appropriate command button

To remove emphasis from text:

▶ Select: The emphasised text

▶ Click: The appropriate command button to deselect the feature

Margin alignment
Format/emphasis

Centre text (between left/right margins)	Press: **Ctrl + E**	Click: The ▤ **Centre** button
Align to the left (ragged right margin)	Press: **Ctrl + L**	Click: The ▤ **Align Left** button
Fully justify (justified right margin)	Press: **Ctrl + J**	Click: The ▤ **Justify** button
Align to the right (ragged left margin)		Click: The ▤ **Align Right** button

Line spacing
Format/emphasis

Single line spacing	Press: **Ctrl + 1**	Select: **Paragraph** from the **Format** menu
Double line spacing	Press: **Ctrl + 2**	Select: **Indents and Spacing**, **Line Spacing**
Add or delete a line space	Press: **Ctrl + 0**	Select: The appropriate line spacing from the drop-down menu
	Press: **Ctrl + 0** again to remove line space	

 Exercise 1C

1.6   Starting with a clear screen, key in the document on the next page. Correct all the words that are incorrectly spelt (those with a dotted line underneath). Use a justified right margin, Times New Roman and font size 12 for the main text and apply the text emphasis where indicated.

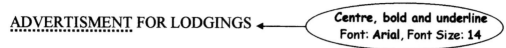

ADVERTISMENT FOR LODGINGS ←——— Centre, bold and underline
Font: Arial, Font Size: 14

In reply to the recent advertisments for temparory board and lodgings for visiting company representatives, I am able to reccomend a small but friendly Guest House close to the town centre. Several of my own buisness clients have used this acommodation before and have experianced it to be more than satisfactory.

Most of the bedrooms come with a seperate bathroom and I beleive their is ample axcess to car parking facilities. The owner is a very responsable lady who offers an extremely flexible service, particularly with meal arrangements. Apparantly, the prices are also very reasonable but it may be worth requesting a definate up-date of room types and financiail details.

Any further coresspondence should be addressed to: ←——— Centre and bold

Mrs Jean Mayberry
Mayberry House   ←——— Centre and italics
Thorne Lane   Font: Arial
BURNLEY BL2 4EU   Font Size: 10

1.7 Use the spelling and grammar tool to check your work, and proofread it carefully yourself as well.

1.8 Save and print your document, using the file name **EX1C**. Check your printout with the printout check at the back of the book. If you find any errors, correct them and print the document again, if necessary.

Change the document line length

You may need to change the format of a document by changing the document line length for the whole of a document or for certain sections only. You can do this by increasing or decreasing the margins, or using the indent facility.

If you are asked to leave a specified amount of horizontal space at any point in a task, you may choose to use either the indent function or alter the margin settings as appropriate.

You should not confuse indenting text with setting left and right margins:

▶ Margins set the overall width of the main text and the amount of space between the main text and the edges of the page.
▶ Indenting moves the text in or out from the margins.

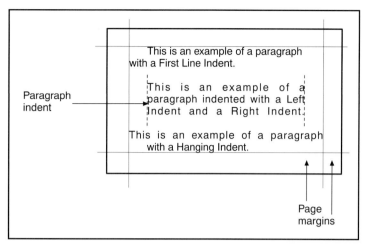

Figure 1.2 Paragraph indent

When you operate the indent feature, the cursor moves to the first pre-set tab stop (usually defaulted to 1.2 cm ($\frac{1}{2}$ in) from the left margin). As you carry on typing, the text will 'wrap around' the indent point until you operate the command to go back to the original left margin.

You can choose to indent the text from both the left and right margins or from the left margin only. It is often more convenient to use the indent function to indent a single paragraph, rather than changing the margins.

 Change margin settings ▶

Mouse/Menu bar method

Select: **Page Setup** from the File menu

The Page Setup dialogue box is displayed on screen.

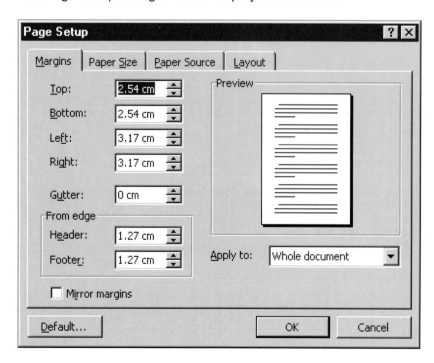

Figure 1.3 Page Setup dialogue box

Click: The **Margins tab**

Key in: The required measurement in the **Left** spin box

Key in: The required measurement in the **Right** spin box

From the **Apply to** drop-down menu: Select: The document portion for the new margin settings

Click: **OK**

Mouse/Ruler markers method

To display the ruler on the document screen:

▶ Select: **Ruler** from the **View** menu

▶ Check: That you are in Page Layout View

▶ Point to: The left or right margin boundary on the horizontal ruler (where the dark grey and white sections of the ruler meet); when the pointer changes to a 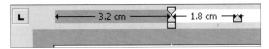 double-headed arrow: Hold down: The mouse button and drag the margin boundary to the required position on the ruler

To see the exact measurement on the ruler:

▶ Hold down: The **Alt** key as you drag the margin boundary

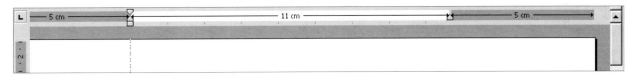

Figure 1.4 Exact ruler measurement

This method also lets you view the **typing line length** measurement on screen:

▶ Hold down: The **Alt** key as you click on the left or right margin boundary or on the indent *(You will see the measurements of the margins, indents and typing line length displayed across the horizontal ruler)*

Figure 1.5 Typing line length

To indent a portion of text
Keyboard

Indent to the next tab stop	Press: **Ctrl + M**
Indent to the previous tab stop	Press: **Ctrl + Shift + M**
Indent as a hanging paragraph	Press: **Ctrl + T** (and press the **Tab** key)
Remove indent and return to standard margins	Press: **Ctrl + Q**

Formatting Tool Bar

Indent to the next tab stop	Click: The **Increase Indent** button
Indent to the previous tab stop	Click: The **Decrease Indent** button

Ruler

To display the horizontal ruler on screen (unless it is already visible):

▶ Select: **Ruler** from the View menu
▶ Check: That you are in Page Layout View
▶ Select: The paragraph(s) you want to indent
▶ Drag: The indent markers to the required position on the horizontal ruler

To set a right indent	Drag ⬠	To set a first line indent	Drag ▽
To set a left indent	Drag ⬡	To set a hanging indent	Drag ⬢

To set a Negative indent, ie scroll into the left margin:

▶ Hold down: The **Shift** key
▶ Drag: The left first line indent marker to the required position
▶ As you drag the margin indent: Hold down: The **Alt** key to see the exact measurement on the ruler

Figure 1.6 Ruler measurement

Menu

To display the horizontal ruler on screen (unless it is already visible):

▶ Select: **Ruler** from the View menu
▶ Check: That you are in Page Layout View
▶ Select: The paragraph(s) you want to indent
▶ Select: **Paragraph** from the Format menu
▶ Select: **Indents and Spacing**

The Indents and Spacing dialogue box is displayed on screen.

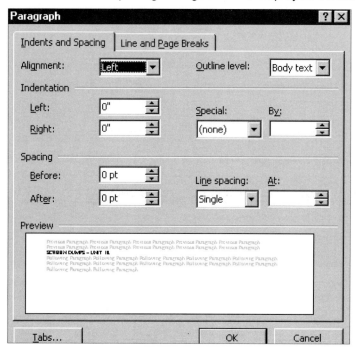

Figure 1.7 Indents and Spacing dialogue box

- ► Select: The paragraph alignment from the **Alignment** drop-down menu
- ► In the **Indentation** boxes: Select or key in: The left and right indent measurements required
- ► Select: **First Line** or **Hanging** indents (or none) from the list in the Special drop-down menu
- ► If the default measurement is not appropriate: Select: An alternative measurement for the first line or hanging indent from the **By** drop-down menu
- ► Click: **OK**

 ## Change the typing line length ►

You may be asked to change the 'typing line length' (or typing line) of a document to a fixed number of characters. This is achieved by insetting the margins or by indenting using the indent function. (It is not always possible in word processing to be completely accurate in this respect and examiners should be aware of this and be lenient in their marking of this feature.)

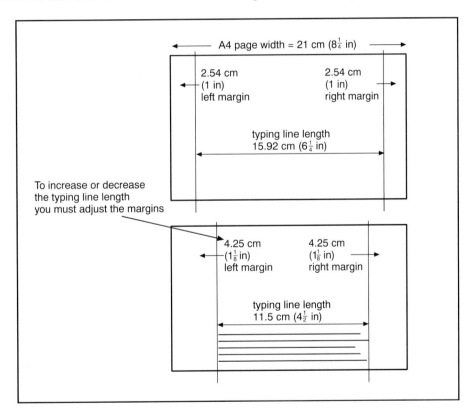

Figure 1.8 Typing line length

The width of an A4 page is 21 cm ($8\frac{1}{4}$ in). The typing line length is the difference between the page width and the two margin measurements. For example, if the left and right margins are both set by default to 2.54 cm (1 in):

width of A4 page	=	21.00 cm ($8\frac{1}{4}$in)
minus left margin	–	2.54 cm (1 in)
minus right margin	–	2.54 cm (1 in)
typing line length	**=**	**15.92 cm ($6\frac{1}{4}$ in)**

To increase or decrease the typing line length, you must adjust the margin settings.

Figure 1.8 shows equal left and right margins but this is not absolutely necessary. Your left margin could be wider than your right, as long as the typing line length is correct. As shown in Figure 1.8, if you were asked to set a typing line length of 11.5 cm ($4\frac{1}{2}$ in) you would need to increase both the left and right margins. You could either increase both margins to 4.25 cm ($1\frac{3}{8}$ in) or you could set a left margin of 5.5 cm ($2\frac{1}{8}$ in) and a right margin of 3 cm ($1\frac{1}{8}$ in).

To change the typing line length for the whole document:

Calculate what the new margin settings need to be in order to give the correct typing line length. Use either the Page Setup method (Mouse and menu, page 14) or the Alt key facility (Mouse and ruler, page 15) to change the margin settings before or after keying in the document. You may even wish to use a combination of the two methods, ie change the left and right margins using the Page Setup method, then check the typing line length on the horizontal ruler using the Alt key facility.

To change the typing line length for part of a document:

Follow the instructions given earlier (To indent a portion of text, p. 15).

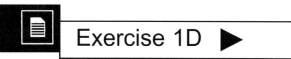

Exercise 1D ▶

1.9   Open the document you saved as **EX1C**. Save it as **EX1D**.

▶ Remove the underline from the main heading but retain the font size.
▶ Remove any centring and align all the text to the left with a ragged right margin.
▶ Use a typing line length of 13 cm ($5\frac{1}{8}$ in)
▶ Indent the name and address at the bottom of the document by 1.27 cm ($\frac{1}{2}$ in).
▶ Use double line spacing for the first two paragraphs only.
▶ Change the font of the address to Times New Roman, font size 12.

1.10   Save your document again (using the same filename). Use Word 97's Print Preview facility to compare your document with the printout check at the back of the book. If the format is not correct, re-read the instructions and amend the format if necessary. If the format is correct, print out a copy of your document.

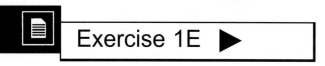

Exercise 1E ▶

1.11   Starting with a clear screen, key in the document on the following page. Correct all the words that are incorrectly spelt – those that are circled. Use a justified right margin, Times New Roman and font size 12 for the main text and apply the text emphasis where indicated.

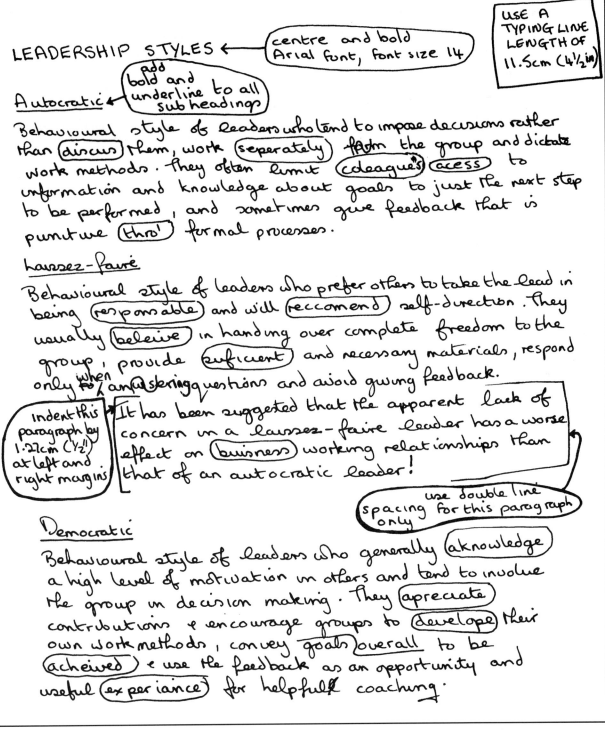

LEADERSHIP STYLES

*centre and bold
Arial font, font size 14*

USE A TYPING LINE LENGTH OF 11.5cm (4½in)

Autocratic

add bold and underline to all sub headings

Behavioural style of leaders who tend to impose decisions rather than (discus) them, work (seperately) from the group and dictate work methods. They often limit (coleague's) (acess) to information and knowledge about goals to just the next step to be performed, and sometimes give feedback that is punitive (thro') formal processes.

Laissez-faire

Behavioural style of leaders who prefer others to take the lead in being (responsable) and will (reccomend) self-direction. They usually (beleive) in handing over complete freedom to the group, provide (suficient) and necessary materials, respond only when (answerring) questions and avoid giving feedback.

Indent this paragraph by 1.27cm (½") at left and right margins

It has been suggested that the apparent lack of concern in a laissez-faire leader has a worse effect on (buisness) working relationships than that of an autocratic leader!

use double line spacing for this paragraph only

Democratic

Behavioural style of leaders who generally (aknowledge) a high level of motivation in others and tend to involve the group in decision making. They (apreciate) contributions & encourage groups to (develope) their own work methods, convey (goals) overall to be (acheived) & use the feedback as an opportunity and useful (experiance) for helpfull coaching.

1.12   Use the spelling and grammar tool to check your work, and proofread it carefully yourself.

1.13   Save your document, using the filename **EX1E** and print one copy. Check your printout with the printout check at the back of the book. If you find any errors, correct them and print again if necessary.

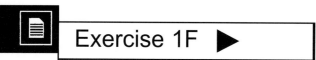

Exercise 1F ▶

1.14 You are now going to use text emphasis to create a standard file for a business memorandum head. You will recall this memo template in Unit 3 when practising business memorandum layout – the purpose of this exercise is to practise using text emphasis for effective display.

Starting a new file, key in the following text, centring both lines and using the text emphasis indicated:

> **ACE BUSINESS SERVICES** ← Arial font size 22 Bold
>
> **MEMORANDUM** ← Arial font size 28 Bold

1.15 Save your document using the filename **Memotemp**.

1.16 Use the Print Preview facility to check your work against the key at the back of the book. If there are any errors, correct them before printing a copy of the document for use in a later unit.

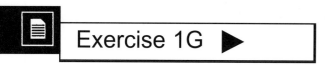

Exercise 1G ▶

1.17 You are now going to use text emphasis to create a standard file for a business letterhead. You will recall this file later in Unit 3 when practising business letter layout – the purpose of this exercise is to practise using text emphasis for effective display.

Starting a new file, key in the following text, centring all lines and using the text emphasis indicated:

> **ACE BUSINESS SERVICES** ← Arial font size 22 Bold
>
> Arial font size 14 → **246 Park View**
> **LEEDS LS1 6RD**
>
> *Tel no: 0113 246589*   *Fax no: 0113 246577* ← Arial font size 10 Italic

1.18 Save your document using filename **Lettertemp**.

1.19 Use the Print Preview facility to check your work against the key at the back of the book. If there are any errors, correct them before printing a copy of the document for use in a later unit.

1.20 Exit the program if you have finished working or clear your screen and continue straight on to the next unit.

▶ Multi-page documents

By the end of Unit 2, you should have learnt how to:

▶ identify and correct grammatical and punctuation errors
▶ expand correctly common abbreviations
▶ amend documents in accordance with correction signs
▶ insert additional blocks of text into existing documents
▶ insert page numbering on continuation sheets
▶ identify and correct inconsistencies in text
▶ insert accented letters in international text.

Typescript containing grammatical and punctuation errors

As you are keying in text, you should make sure that what you are typing makes sense. You should watch out for:

▶ errors of agreement, eg when the noun and the verb in a sentence do not agree
▶ incorrect use or omission of punctuation, eg apostrophes
▶ incorrect use of punctuation in documents using the fully-blocked, open punctuation style
▶ omission of capital letters for proper nouns and at the beginning of sentences.

Examples
Errors of agreement

> The difference between the two word-processing programs were demonstrated by the supervisor

should be keyed in as:

The difference between the two word processing programs was demonstrated by the supervisor

▶ There are two programs but only one difference.

Incorrect use of apostrophe

> Its too late now to go to the shops' as they close at 5.30 pm on Thursday's

should be keyed in as:

It's too late now to go to the shops as they close at 5.30 pm on Thursdays.

▶ *It's* is a shortened form of It is: the apostrophe shows that the letter **i** has been omitted.

▶ *Shops* does not require an apostrophe after the **s** as this would indicate possession, eg the shops' awnings were brightly coloured.

▶ *Thursdays* does not require an apostrophe before the **s** as this would indicate possession, eg Thursday's delivery was late.

Further information on the use of the apostrophe is included in *Advancing Word 97 for Windows.*

Incorrect use of capital letters

> We found barbara's letter. it was in a pile of mail in one of the Offices.

should be keyed in as:

We found Barbara's letter. It was in a pile of mail in one of the offices.

▶ *Barbara* should have a capital letter as it is a proper noun.

▶ *It* should have a capital **I** as it is the first letter of the first word in a sentence.

▶ *Offices* does not require a capital letter as it is not a special office.

Grammar Tool

Word 97 will check your document for possible grammar and style errors and offer suggestions for correcting them. If you know your grammar is weak, this is a useful facility, but still does not replace personal proofreading skills. Sometimes it can create confusion by suggesting unnecessary amendments to sentences.

The Grammar check facility can be 'switched off' by selecting **Tools** from the menu, **Options**, **Spelling & Grammar** and then clicking in the **'Check grammar as you type'** box and the **'Check grammar with spelling'** box to remove the ✔.

Typescript containing abbreviations ▶

Text authors often use abbreviations when writing out copy which is to be processed by a word processor operator. In the work situation, you would quickly get used to individual authors' 'shorthand'. The following list shows some abbreviations you can expect to come across in intermediate examinations such as RSA's Stage II Text Processing Awards. You should key in these words in full whenever you see them, unless otherwise instructed. In the RSA examinations, open punctuation is used so there are no 'full stops' after the abbreviations shown on the following page.

a/c(s)	account(s)	opp(s)	opportunity/ies
approx	approximately	org	organisation
cat(s)	catalogue(s)	poss	possible
co(s)	company/ies	ref(d)	refer(red)
dr	dear	ref(s)	reference(s)
gntee(s)	guarantee(s)	sec(s)	secretary/ies
immed	immediate(ly)	sig(s)	signature(s)
info	information	temp	temporary
misc	miscellaneous	yr(s)	year(s)
mfr(s)	manufacturer(s)	yr(s)	your(s)
necy	necessary		

Some abbreviations should be kept as they are, for example:

etc	eg	ie	NB
PS	plc	Ltd	& (in company names)

Note: Word 97's spelling check may suggest that some abbreviations such as ie and eg should have full stops, for example i.e. and e.g. In word processing, it is now common practice to omit the full stops in such instances. You can add the abbreviations without full stops to the spelling memory as follows.

▶ Key in the abbreviations and run spelling check.
▶ When the spellchecker stops on the abbreviation, click the **Add** button.
▶ Word will add the new form of the abbreviation to its memory and will not suggest full stops for it again.

You will also be expected to key in the following words in full.

▶ days of the week, eg Wednesday, Thursday
▶ months of the year, eg February, September
▶ words in addresses, eg Grove, Drive, Crescent
▶ complimentary closes, eg Yours faithfully/sincerely

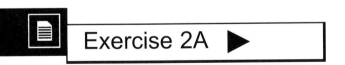

Exercise 2A ▶

2.1 Starting a new document, key in the text on the next page, correcting the circled spelling and grammatical errors and expanding the abbreviations as you go along.

CUSTOMER INFORMATION ← Underline

PLACING AN ORDER ← Bold

It is our intention to (acheive) our target of (suppling) all of our (customer's) with all of the goods ordered on the date promised. You can help us to help you (buy) preparing yr order before telephoning. If you need further info on any of our products, we (recomend) that you ref to our co's Customer Information Service. (we) can give an immed response to most queries. If necy, we will check details with mfrs and call you back within approx 2 to 3 (hours;)

<u>By telephone</u>

Ring our Order Hotline number when you have (prepare) a list of yr needs. Our operator will ask you for the following info: cat number, colour or size, description, price per unit, quantity, customer number. If our lines are busy, you will be asked to leave yr customer number and telephone number. We will call you back as soon as we (possible) can.

<u>By fax</u>

If you have (acces) to a fax (machine ,) we would be pleased to receive yr order in this way to save you time and money. We supply order forms in the form of a pad printed to ensure no details (is) omitted.

Please do remember to tell us if you require (deliver) to an address which is different to the one registered on our customer database and which is normally used for all (correspondance.)

If you need to contact us after office hours, our answerphone will record yr message and/or your order.

2.2 Proofread your work carefully. If you find any errors, correct them.

2.3 Save your document as **EX2A**. There is no need to print at this stage.

Typescript containing correction signs

A word processor operator often has to make amendments to documents after the text author has proofread them. You will already be familiar with basic text-correction signs. In this Unit, you will learn additional correction signs. The following list shows all the correction signs you can expect to come across in intermediate examinations such as RSA's Stage II Text Processing Awards.

Correction Sign	Meaning
	Start a new paragraph here
	Run on – join paragraphs or sections of text
	Insert a word (or words) here. The words may be immediately above the insertion sign or circled and joined to the insertion sign by an arrow or line
	Transpose horizontally
	Transpose vertically
	Close up – ie don't leave a space
twowords	Leave a space – ie split the words at this point
word	Let it be. Key in or retain the word(s) with the dashed underline

Insert additional text into an existing document

Text authors often require additional text to be incorporated into a document while it is being prepared or after it has been printed. In the RSA Stage II Part 1 Text Processing examination, the invigilator will simulate this by issuing an extra sheet of paper to candidates between 15 to 30 minutes after the start of the examination. The sheet will contain text which is to be included in one of the examination documents.

Make sure that you insert the additional text in the correct position. There will be a hand-written note to indicate where this should be.

2.4   Retrieve the document you saved as **EX2A**, save as **EX2B** and amend the text as shown below.

CUSTOMER INFORMATION → centre

justified margins please

change to double line-spacing

PLACING ~~AN~~ ORDERS

It is our intention to achieve our target of supplying all of our customers with all of the goods ordered on the date promised. You can help us to help you by preparing your order before telephoning. [If you need further information on any of our products, we recommend that you refer to our company's Customer Information Service. We can give an immediate response to most queries. If necessary, we will check details with ~~manufacturers~~ and call you back within approximately 2 to 3 hours.
Suppliers

By telephone

requirements

Ring our Order Hotline number when you have prepared a list of your ~~needs~~. Our operator will ask you for the following information: catalogue number, colour or size, description, price per unit, quantity, customer number. /If our lines are busy, you will be asked to leave your customer number and telephone number. We will call you back as soon as we possibly can. This means that you will not be wasting valuable time.

By fax

If you have access to a fax machine, we would be pleased to receive your order in this way to save you time and money. We supply order forms in the form of a pad printed to ensure no details are omitted.

Please do remember to tell us if you require delivery to an address which is different to the one registered on our customer database and which is normally used for all correspondence.

9.00am to 5.30pm Mon to Fri,

If you need to contact us after office hours, our answerphone will record your message and/or your order.

* Insert extra paragraphs here
Delivery

Ref to our map (on seperate page at front of cat) to determine the day of the week when deliveries are made to yr area. The minimum order amount is shown on this page. We feel sure you will appreciate that an order must be sufficently large to justify
BOLD free delivery.

2.5 Insert the following text at the point indicated. Save the document and read the sections on pagination and page numbering before going on to step 2.6 to complete the exercise.

> Terms
>
> Pre-paid by 1 week or cash on delivery. Bank or trade ⟨firms⟩ refs will take about 10 days; after this clearance/we will accept cheques.
>
> Returned or re-presented ⟨checks⟩ will be charged at £15 on each occasion. /we reserve the right not to accept orders, and all goods remain our property until they have been/are paid for.
>
> Yr signature on delivery ⟨aknowledges⟩ ⟨reciept⟩ of all the goods shown on the invoice at the price shown given and in good condition. Claims can be accepted only on quality. ⟨concerns regarding⟩ Contact the Customer Info Service in the unlikely event of such a problem. We ✓ will do our best to ~~sort out~~ ~~resolve~~ the issue to yr satisfaction.

Pagination for continuation sheets ▶

When you are keying in a long document of several pages, Word 97 automatically inserts 'soft' page breaks for you. In 'Normal View' mode, a page break is shown by a horizontal dotted line on the screen with the words **Page Break** in the centre of the line. The printer will start a new page at this point. However, you may need to insert new page breaks yourself in a specific place – these are often called 'hard' page breaks. Page breaks should be inserted in sensible places within a document so that it is easy to read. When paginating (inserting page breaks):

✗   The complimentary close of a letter (Yours...) should never be the *only* text on the last page.

✗   You should not divide a word between one page and the next.

✗   You should not leave only the first line of a paragraph at the bottom of a page (a 'widow').

✗   You should not carry forward only the last line of a paragraph on to the next page (an 'orphan').

Widow/orphan control
Word 97 allows you to automatically avoid widows and orphans. Check that Word is defaulted to do this:

▶   Select: **Format**, **Paragraph**, **Line and Page Breaks**

▶   Check that the **Widow/Orphan** box is ticked

All other boxes should be blank.

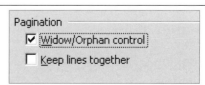

Figure 2.1 Widow/orphan control

Insert a new page break

Position the cursor where you want to insert the page break:

Keyboard	Mouse and menu
Press: **Ctrl** + ↵ (return)	Select: **Insert**, **Break**, **Page break**, **OK**

Page numbering for continuation sheets

It is customary to number the pages of a multi-page document so that readers can follow the page sequence more easily. Word 97 has a page numbering command that allows you to set page numbering once so that page numbers will appear automatically on all pages of the document.

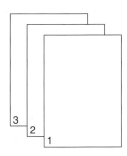

In some instances you may not want the page number to appear on page one, eg the first page of a multi-page letter is not usually numbered. You can tell Word 97 not to show the number on the first page where appropriate. However, in RSA examinations you will not incur a fault for numbering the first page.

Figure 2.2 Page numbering

Insert page numbers

Keyboard	Mouse and menu
Position the cursor: At the required position	Select: **Page Numbers** from the **Insert** menu
Press: **Alt** + **Shift** + **P** *(the page number appears on screen)*	The Page Numbers dialogue box is displayed on screen.
Note: You have to repeat the instruction on each page so this method is not entirely satisfactory. It is better to use the menu method.	

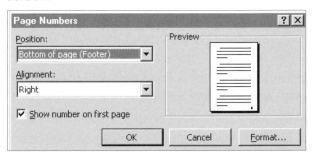

Figure 2.3 Page Numbers dialogue box

Page numbering offers a choice of:

▶ **Position**;
▶ **Alignment**; and
▶ **Show number on first page**.
▶ The Preview box allows you to see the position of the page number.

Note: Page numbers only show on screen in **Page Layout View** and **Print Preview**.

Select from the page numbers dialogue box as appropriate:

Button	Action
Position	Select position on page *vertically* – **Bottom** (footer) or **Top** (header)
Alignment	Select position on page *horizontally* – **Left**, **Right**, or **Centre** (**Inside** and **Outside** are used with binding margins, ie facing pages)
Show number on first page	Remove the ✔ if you don't want a number to appear on the first page (eg on a multi-page letter)

Preview	Displays the page number in the chosen position
Format	Allows a different format of page number to be selected, ie Arabic, roman numerals, letters
Page numbering	Allows you to decide on the page numbering sequence

2.6 Insert a page break in a sensible place in the document and insert page numbering so that both pages will show a number at the bottom centre.

2.7 Proofread your work carefully, comparing it with the printout check at the back of the book. If you find any errors, correct them. Save your document (as **EX2B** still) and print one copy.

Consistency of presentation ▶

Measurements, weights, times and money

You should always be consistent in the way you present information within a document. The following are examples of points you should watch out for.

Be consistent in the use of an abbreviation to represent a measurement or weight, such as mm, cm, ft, in, kg, oz, lb. For example, don't key in **30"** in one place and **30 in** somewhere else in the document. Be consistent – use either **"** or **in** but not a mixture of the two.

You may leave one space before the abbreviation or no spaces but you must be consistent. For example, don't key in **46kg** in one place and **46 kg** somewhere else in the document.

Stick to the 12-hour clock or the 24-hour clock when showing times. For example, don't key in **1600 hrs** in one place and **7.30 am** somewhere else in the document. Be consistent in the use of **pm**, **o'clock**, **hrs**.

When using an abbreviation for currency (eg **$**, **£**, **DM**, **F**), stick to one method of presentation. For example, don't key in **£15** in one place and **£12.50** somewhere else in the document. Both amounts should show the pence – (**£15.00** and **£12.50**). You should use either **£** or **p** but not both together in one amount – **£0.50p** is wrong. Don't key in **FF100** in one place and **100 French francs** somewhere else in the document.

Words and figures

Be consistent in the way you present numbers within a document. For example, don't key in **40 miles** in one place and **fifty-five miles** somewhere else in the document. Look through the text first and decide on words or figures. Think about these two examples.

▶ 1,234,650 is difficult to express in words
▶ 1 looks strange as the first word of a sentence.

Other possible inconsistencies

Be consistent in using the dash (-) or the hyphen (-) between words and symbols. The keyboard symbol is the same, the spacing either side of the symbol is different. (A dash 'separates' words and has one space before and after. A hyphen 'joins' words and has no spaces before and after.) Don't key in **4 - 6** in one place and **16-21** somewhere else in the document. Also, don't key in **4 to 6** in one place and **16-21** somewhere else in the document. The word **to** can also be used in **3 to 4 weeks'** time and **Tuesday to Thursday**. Don't key in **Friday - Sunday** in one place and **Monday to Wednesday** somewhere else in the document.

Take care in the use of initial capitals for words – it is not necessary for words which are not proper nouns ('names') to have a capital letter unless they start a sentence. The words **personnel** and **organisations** do not need to have capital letters in the following sentence:

We sent invitations to the Personnel departments in all local Organisations.

It should be keyed in as:

We sent invitations to the personnel departments in all local organisations.

Be consistent in the presentation of percentages. For example, don't key in **50%** in one place and **50 per cent** somewhere else in the document.

When keying in words which can be spelt in two different ways, make sure all occurrences match. For example, don't key in **organise** in one place and **organize** somewhere else in the document.

Be consistent in the amount of space you leave after punctuation. For example, don't leave **1 space** after a full stop in one place and **2 spaces** after a full stop somewhere else in the document. Don't mix open and full punctuation styles in business letters – see Unit 3 (p. 36).

Be consistent in the amount of line space between separate parts of a document, eg between paragraphs and after headings. It is normal practice to leave at least one clear line. It is not always necessary, however, to leave a clear line space between items which are listed or numbered.

You should standardise the layout of any document which you are producing. For example, don't mix paragraph styles (eg keep them all blocked to the left or all indented) and make all headings the same style (eg all in capitals or all in lower case and underlined).

Exercise 2C ▶

2.8 Key in the following document, ensuring consistency of presentation throughout.

RENTINET → *centre, bold*

Your gateway to the world ← *change to CAPS*

For just £14.00 (+ VAT) per month plus an initial payment of only £25 (plus VAT), you can be instantly connected to the rest of the world!

With over thirty million users world-wide, the Internet is growing at an ⟨unbeleivable⟩ 12% per month. Realise the potential for your organisation!

Setting-up Package (£25 + vat at 17.5 per cent = £29.38)
Sign-up registration Charge
Set-up of Internet a/c
configuration of computer, and Modem ← *delete comma*
Fully-licensed software

Save 10 % if you pay for 1 year in advance - £ saving
* Insert extra paragraphs here later
Let us take all the worry out of your ~~technical~~ technological information and communications systems.
SYSTEM CHECK ← *make all headings like this one*

Your IBM-compatible PC will need:
use this style for Megabytes throughout

Windows 3.1	4 Mb RAM	5 Mb free hard disk space
Windows 95	8mB RAM	20 mb free hard disk space
Apple Macintosh	8Mb RAM	5 MB free hard disk space

2.9 Proofread your work carefully. If you find any errors, correct them.

2.10 Save your document as **EX2C** and print one copy. Compare your work with the printout check at the back of the book and correct any errors.

Add characters not available on the keyboard ▶

You may sometimes be required to reproduce symbols such as:

▶ fractions, eg $\frac{1}{4}$ $1\frac{1}{2}$ $6\frac{3}{4}$
▶ accented letters, eg à é ñ ä.

Fractions

Word 97 automatically creates common fractions such as $\frac{1}{4}, \frac{1}{2}, \frac{3}{4}$ as you key in the numbers with the oblique stroke (solidus) between them: for example, if you key in 1/4 Word 97 will convert this to $\frac{1}{4}$. Some other fractions such as 1/3 and 2/5 are not automatically converted in this way but are available by using the Insert Symbol function and selecting a font style which contains the fraction you require.

Accented letters

You can access accented letters by using the Insert Symbol function and selecting a font style which contains the accented letter you require.

 Insert Symbol function ▶

▶ Select: **Insert** from the file menu
▶ Select: **Symbol** from the drop-down menu
▶ Select: The **Symbols** tab on the dialogue box
▶ Select: (**normal text**) in the **Font** box

The Symbol dialogue box is displayed on screen.

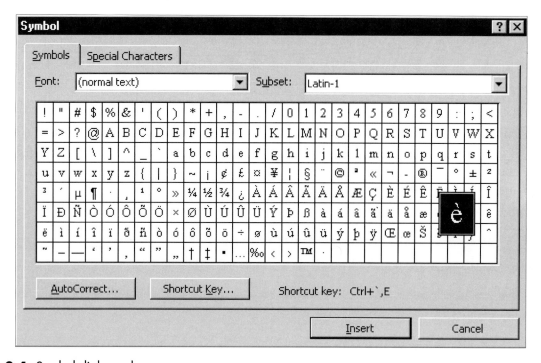

Figure 2.4 Symbol dialogue box

In Figure 2.4, the lower case letter **e** with a grave accent has been selected by clicking on the character. This allows you to check that you have chosen the correct character.

Note: Also displayed are the shortcut (combination) keys you could use to reproduce the same character.

▶ Click: **Insert** to select this character and insert it into the text
▶ Click: **Close** to return to the document

Shortcut keys

You can also apply accents to text in other languages using the **combination keys** function (ie pressing two or more keys simultaneously)

Figure 2.5 shows the keys to be used to reproduce accented letters. (This table can be found in the **Help** menu index under **International characters**.)

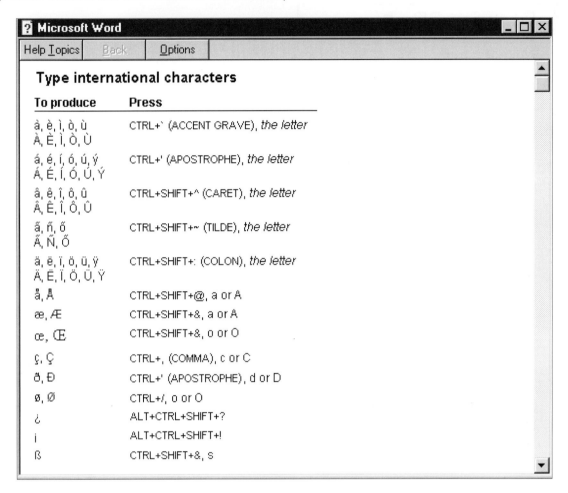

Figure 2.5 International characters table

For example, when keying in the word **fricassée**, to produce the **é**:

▶ Press **Ctrl + '** (apostrophe)
▶ Press: **e**

To insert an accent with an upper case letter:

▶ Press: The key combination
▶ Press: **Shift** + the letter

For example, when keying in the word **NOËL**, to produce the **Ë**:

▶ Press: **Ctrl + Shift + :** (colon)
▶ Press: **Shift + E**

Other symbols

Note: You will find many other useful symbols such as ticks, fractions, arrows, etc by investigating the different fonts in the Symbol dialogue box.

Some examples are: ß § © Ÿ ℞ ⅔ œ ✓ ♥ ✿ Σ ➡ Æ

Experiment with these when you have some spare time. However, remember to confine your use of some of the more unusual symbols to your own work – do not use them in examinations!

 Exercise 2D ▶

2.11 Starting with a clear screen, key in the following memorandum, ensuring consistency of presentation throughout.

To: Elisabeth Händel, Advertising Unit
From: Adèle Mélin, Marketing Unit
Date:

CAPS (Retinet) Centre

As discussed earlier today, I enclose hard copy for use in designing the flyers for the launch of the above Centre.

Please let me have the drafts for checking in the following formats so that I can decide on the most effective size and cost:

A5   149mm × 210 mm   80 gsm   écru

A4   210mm by 297 mm   100gsm   orange

I also enclose the text on disk to save time.

                                        design   range
I look (foreword) to seeing your ideas and a selection of suitable graphics in due course.
                    pictures   asap

Encs

As there are only 3½ weeks to go until the Centre launch I would appreciate it if you could give this matter your urgent attention.

2.12 Proofread your work carefully. If you find any errors, correct them.

2.13 Save your document as **EX2D** and print one copy. Compare your work with the printout check at the back of the book, checking particularly that the accented letters have been correctly reproduced.

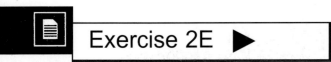

Exercise 2E ▶

2.14 Retrieve the document **EX2C**. Save as **EX2E** and add the following text at the point which was indicated in the copy at step 2.8 (p. 31). Ensure consistency of presentation with the remainder of the document.

> The RENTINET Centre is open for setting-up from
> 9 am to 6.00 pm   Mon-Thurs
> 9 am — 8 pm   Fri to Sat
>
> Just bring your PC (along) – we'll do the rest.
> (Booking advised — Tel: Matthiäs Schneider on
> 01234-1098765)
>
> We realize you may not be able to leave the office —
> we'll come to you.
>
> FREE setting-up session within 8-mile radius. £15
> fee for nine to 15-miles radius.
>
> We realise ~~that~~ you may need help – the RENTINET
> Centre will be your <u>local</u> advice point — always
> ⊘ ~~there~~ when you need us.
>   there
> Still teetering on the brink? ⋙ ᵀtake the plunge.
> RENTINET is yr gntee of a safe landing!

2.15 Proofread your work carefully. If you find any errors, correct them.

2.16 Save your document and print one copy. Compare your work with the printout check at the back of the book.

2.17 Exit the program if you have finished working or continue straight on to the next unit.

unit 3
▶ Producing business documents

By the end of Unit 3, you should have learnt how to:

▶ produce a business letter and a memorandum on pre-printed forms and templates using open punctuation and fully blocked style and with special marks and enclosure marks

▶ confirm facts by locating information from another document and including it where indicated

Note: Although Word 97 has an in-built **Letter Wizard** facility, it is not entirely suitable for RSA examination purposes.

 ## Business documents – letters and memos

In the RSA Stage II Part 1 Text Processing examination you will be expected to produce a business letter and a memorandum either by printing on to a pre-printed form, or by using a template file. You will have already learnt most of the requirements at Stage I, but some details are repeated here as a reminder and for ease of reference.

 ## Business letter layout

A business letter is written on behalf of an organisation and is printed or typed on the organisation's own letterhead. An attractive letterhead gives a good impression of the organisation and contains all relevant details such as telephone and fax numbers. Only the name and address of the addressee (recipient of the letter) have to be typed because the sender's details are already printed on the letterhead. The company's letterhead may be stored as a template file (blueprint) on your computer – you can recall it whenever you need to complete a company letter.

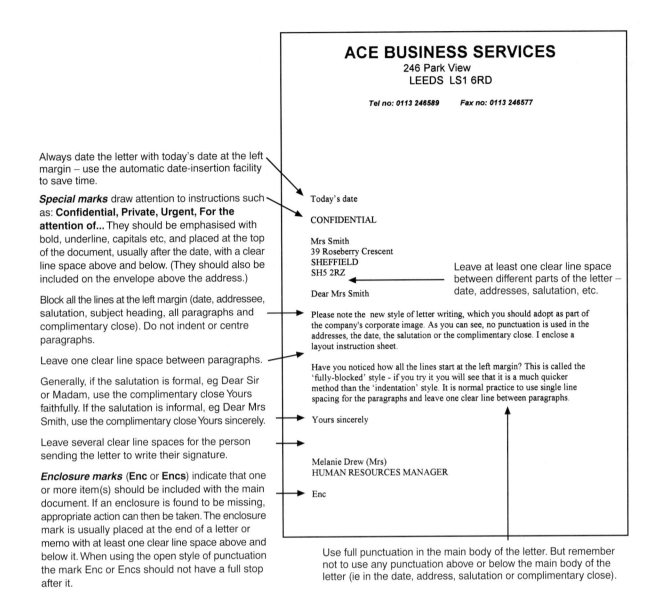

Always date the letter with today's date at the left margin – use the automatic date-insertion facility to save time.

Special marks draw attention to instructions such as: **Confidential, Private, Urgent, For the attention of...** They should be emphasised with bold, underline, capitals etc, and placed at the top of the document, usually after the date, with a clear line space above and below. (They should also be included on the envelope above the address.)

Block all the lines at the left margin (date, addressee, salutation, subject heading, all paragraphs and complimentary close). Do not indent or centre paragraphs.

Leave one clear line space between paragraphs.

Generally, if the salutation is formal, eg Dear Sir or Madam, use the complimentary close Yours faithfully. If the salutation is informal, eg Dear Mrs Smith, use the complimentary close Yours sincerely.

Leave several clear line spaces for the person sending the letter to write their signature.

Enclosure marks (**Enc** or **Encs**) indicate that one or more item(s) should be included with the main document. If an enclosure is found to be missing, appropriate action can then be taken. The enclosure mark is usually placed at the end of a letter or memo with at least one clear line space above and below it. When using the open style of punctuation the mark Enc or Encs should not have a full stop after it.

ACE BUSINESS SERVICES
246 Park View
LEEDS LS1 6RD

Tel no: 0113 246589   Fax no: 0113 246577

Today's date

CONFIDENTIAL

Mrs Smith
39 Roseberry Crescent
SHEFFIELD
SH5 2RZ

Dear Mrs Smith

Leave at least one clear line space between different parts of the letter – date, addresses, salutation, etc.

Please note the new style of letter writing, which you should adopt as part of the company's corporate image. As you can see, no punctuation is used in the addresses, the date, the salutation or the complimentary close. I enclose a layout instruction sheet.

Have you noticed how all the lines start at the left margin? This is called the 'fully-blocked' style – if you try it you will see that it is a much quicker method than the 'indentation' style. It is normal practice to use single line spacing for the paragraphs and leave one clear line between paragraphs.

Yours sincerely

Melanie Drew (Mrs)
HUMAN RESOURCES MANAGER

Enc

Use full punctuation in the main body of the letter. But remember not to use any punctuation above or below the main body of the letter (ie in the date, address, salutation or complimentary close).

 ## Use pre-printed forms or templates

In the Stage II examination you will be asked to print business documents using either a pre-printed form or a template file stored on the computer. Both methods are described here to enable you to choose the one you feel most comfortable with or which is accessible to you.

Using a pre-printed form

In Word 97 the top margin is usually set by default to 2.54 cm (1 in). When printing on a pre-printed form, the top margin on the first page only should be increased to accommodate the printed heading. (Second and subsequent pages are usually printed on plain paper.) You may need to measure the depth of the pre-printed heading on the form you intend to use, and experiment to find the top margin measurement required – you should leave one or two clear line spaces after the heading. Make sure you know how to insert headed paper into the paper-feed tray of your printer so that the document is printed in the correct position.

To alter the top margin to leave space for a pre-printed form heading:

One-page documents

▶ Select: **File**, **Page Setup**, **Margins** (from the menu)

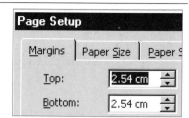

Figure 3.1 Page Setup dialogue box – default settings

▶ In the **Top** box: Notice: The default top margin is normally set at 2.54 cm (1 in)

▶ To replace this with the extra measurement needed, either select or overtype with the required measurement

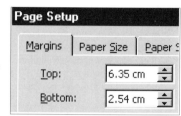

Figure 3.2 Page Setup dialogue box – extra measurement

▶ Select: **Whole Document** from the **Apply to** box

▶ Click: **OK**

Multi-page documents

▶ Repeat the above procedure for the page on which you want to leave extra space – usually page 1

▶ Then, to revert to a normal top margin for all subsequent pages:

▶ Position the cursor: At the bottom of the page which carries the extra heading space

▶ Select: **File**, **Page Setup**, **Margins**

▶ In the **Top** box, select or key in: 2.54 cm (1 in) – or an alternative standard top margin measurement

▶ Select: **This point forward** from the **Apply to** box

▶ Click: **OK**

Note: This ensures that the increased top margin measurement is only set for the page with the pre-printed heading on it – all other pages in the document follow standard top margin settings. It is often better to carry out this procedure after keying in the document but before inserting page breaks.

Using a template file

Templates are often used in business to give a consistent look to the company's documents. A template is a blueprint for specific text, graphics and formatting which will always appear in a document. Memos are a good example of template use as they contain the company name, standard headings, a date field, and place holders to indicate where you type the text.

Note: Word 97 does have a set of templates that you can use as they are or adapt. However, these require saving in a different format. For the purposes of this book and the elementary examination requirements, therefore, you will save your template files in the normal way.

After retrieving your original template file, and before keying in additional details, you should always ensure that you give the second document a different filename. This means that you will not 'overwrite' your template file and you will then be able to retrieve and use the template blueprint over and over again.

To create a template:

▶ Key in: Only those details you want to re-appear every time you open the template file

▶ Save: The file in the normal way as a Word 97 document using a relevant filename, eg **letterhead** or **memohead**.

To open/retrieve a template for use:

▶ Select: **Open** from the **File** menu and open/retrieve your template file in the normal way

▶ Select: **Save As** from the **File** menu

▶ Enter: A different filename for your second document so that you don't overwrite your template blueprint

▶ Add: The rest of the information to the template. For example, if you have retrieved a memohead, key in the rest of the details for the memo. Resave your document to include the added text

 Exercise 3A ▶

3.1 To complete the letter, you will need to open **Lettertemp**, the letterhead template file you saved in Unit 1. The **Ace Business Services** letterhead should now appear on the screen ready for you to complete the rest of the details. Before keying anything in, select the **Save As** command from the **File** menu (so that you don't overwrite your letter template file) and save the file as **EX3A**.

3.2 Key in the rest of the letter from the manuscript copy below.

Note: Before keying in any additional details, you will need to re-set the font to Times New Roman, font size 12. You may also need to alter the margin alignment.

Our ref: SM/24P

Décor - 8
36 Newberry Ave
LEEDS
LS2 3TW

Mark the letter:
FOR THE ATTENTION
OF BRIAN WADSWORTH

Dr Sirs

We (was) very pleased with the decorating work which you carried out last year on our conference suite.

(In (accnowledgement) of this, we wish to advise you that there/an will be opp in the near future for you to tender for some work to be under taken in our new training unit. [I will be inviting several firms to (inspected) the premises e provide us with an estimate for the costs of decorating this new (acomodation). There will also be an opp for you to meet my (coleague), Deborah Pickles, who is our Training Manager and who will provide you with more info about our (requirement's).

I (expects) to hold a (meetings) at the beginning of this next ⊘ month and would be grateful if you could contact me with when you would be available on the reply slip enclosed.

confirm the dates

Yrs ffly

Steven Murgatroyd
ASSISTANT PREMISES OFFICER

3.3 Resave your document and print one copy. Check your printout with the key at the back of the book. If you find any errors, retrieve the document and correct them.

Note: If Spellchecker stops on the enclosure mark, **Enc** or **Encs**, and prompts you to add a full stop, you can simply **Add** the open punctuation version to Spellchecker's memory so that it does not query it again.

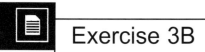

Exercise 3B ▶

3.4 If you cannot access the printer, complete Exercise 3B using the template file, as you did for Exercise 3A. Otherwise, open **Lettertemp**, the file you saved in Unit 1. Print out a copy. Measure the depth of the pre-printed letter heading from the top of the page to the bottom of the heading text and allow for 2 or 3 clear line spaces after it. In total, this should be approximately 6.35 cm ($2\frac{1}{2}$ in). You are going to print Exercise 3B directly on to this pre-printed form in step 3.6.

3.5 Close the file **Lettertemp**. Starting a new file, key in the following letter, using the line spacing shown.

Mark the letter: URGENT

Dr Mr Shaw

I have recently recieved a brochure catalogue of yr range of office furniture. As we are refurbishing the company' new training unit I wonder if it would be poss for me to visited yr premises in order to view the different ranges more closely and to inspect the appearance and quality. I will need yr assurance that any items ordered would be delivered within the next six eight weeks.

Also, you do not indicate in yr correspondance whether discounts would be available for large orders, or the time period for any extended gntee. Perhaps you could contact my sec, Marjorie Wallace, to arrange a suitable time for me to visit your co, preferably within the next two weeks. Marjories' telephone extension number is 237. It would be helpful, in the mean time, if you could forwards some fabric samples from yr standard range of office chairs in the stamped addressed pre-paid envelope enclosed.

in the near future
I look forward to hearing from you shortly.

yrs scly
Deborah Pickles
TRAINING MANAGER

Address the letter to:
Mr Brian Shaw, Strand Furniture Supplies, 3 Merton Rd, BRADFORD, BD17 4RW

3.6 Following the instructions given previously, alter the top margin so that the body of the document does not 'overprint' on top of the pre-printed letter heading. Remember, you will probably need to enter a setting of approximately 6.35 cm ($2\frac{1}{2}$ in) for the top margin in order to allow for several clear line spaces after the letter heading text.

3.7 Save your document using filename **EX3B**.

3.8 Insert the pre-printed letterhead form (ie, the document **Lettertemp** which you printed out at step 3.4) correctly into your printer. Print the document **EX3B** directly onto the pre-printed letterhead. Check your printout with the key at the back of the book. If you find any errors, retrieve the document and correct them.

 ## Memorandum

A memorandum is a document sent 'internally' to convey information to people who work in the same organisation.

At the top of the document, it is customary to enter the name of the person **From** whom the document is being sent and that of the person **To** whom it is being sent, as well as a **Reference**, the **Date** of sending and usually a **Subject Heading**. There is no complimentary close in a memorandum.

You should always insert the date, even if there are no specific instructions to do so – this will be expected of you in the RSA examination. Some people like to sign or initial their memos but this is not absolutely necessary.

Organisations have different ways of aligning and setting out the items on the memo. Two acceptable versions are shown in Figure 3.3.

> **Ace Business Services**
> **MEMORANDUM**
>
> **From:** Sender   **Ref:**   AZ456
>
> **To:**   Receiver   **Date:**   today's
>
> SUBJECT HEADING
>
> Study the layout and spacing of the top part of the memo carefully.
>
> Type the body of the memo in single-line spacing with a clear line space between paragraphs.

> **Ace Business Services**
> **MEMORANDUM**
>
> **From:** Sender
> **To:**   Receiver
> **Ref:**   AZ456
> **Date:**   today's

Figure 3.3 Memorandum layout

 ## Confirming facts

As part of the examination, you will be asked to insert additional information into a document. This information will be found in another document. (At work you would be expected to consult paper files, computer databases, etc.) Take notice of the text you are keying in so that you will be able to select the correct piece of information to make your document accurate.

Automatic date insertion

Word will insert the current date in letters and memoranda, as follows:

Keyboard	Mouse/Menu
Press: **Alt + Shift + D**	Position the pointer: In the place for the date to be inserted
	Select: **Insert** from the menu bar
	Select: **Date and Time**

The Date and Time dialogue box is displayed on the screen.

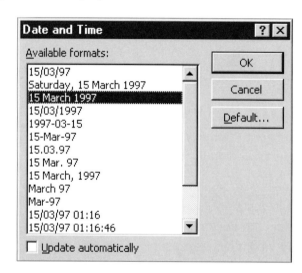

Figure 3.4 The Date and Time dialogue box

▶ Word displays a selection of available date formats
▶ In the UK the third style is usually adopted for letters and memos, ie 15 March 1997
▶ Click: On the date style that you want to insert
▶ Check: That the **Update automatically** box does not have a tick in it (if it does, Word 97 would automatically update the date or time whenever you print the document – sometimes this would be useful)
▶ Click: **OK**

Note: To save making changes when using the keyboard shortcut (**Alt + Shift + D**, you can select the date style as the default style by clicking on **Default** instead of **OK**.

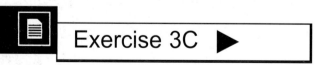 Exercise 3C ▶

3.9 To complete the memo, you will need to open **Memotemp**, the memo template file you saved in Unit 1. The **Ace Business Services** memo template should now appear on the screen ready for you to complete with the rest of the details. So that you don't overwrite your memo template file, select **Save As** from the **File** menu and save the file as **EX3C**.

3.10 Key in the rest of the letter from the manuscript copy on the following page.

Note: Before keying in any additional details, you will need to re-set the font to Times New Roman, font size 12. You may also need to alter the margin alignment.

From: Deborah Pickles, Training Manager
To: Steven Murgatroyd, (insert job title from Exercise 3A)
Ref: SM/864

I am writing with ref to our recent discussions relating to (to be housed in the old staff lounge) the proposal for a new co training unit. The steering (Comitee) has prepared a (reports) on ~~this~~ the details and a copy (are) attached.

I would (apreciate) it if you could prepare a (seperate) estimate of all the (expenses) that are likely to be incurred for the (units') refurbishment ~~xx~~ inclusive of all decorations, fittings (and) fixtures, along with any necy structural alterations. [This info is required by Friday (please insert date for Friday of next week), or sooner if poss.

We will, of course, need to obtain proper tenders for the work to be done from reputable orgs.

I understand you have already begun to contact some of the local firms who have been ~~xxxx~~ (reccomended) to us in the past. With regard to the fittings e fixtures, I attach a list of manufacturers with whom we hold accs for you to (contact;)

3.11 Resave your newly completed memo and print one copy. Check your printout with the key at the back of the book. If you find any errors, retrieve the document and correct them.

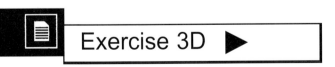

Exercise 3D ▶

3.12 If you cannot access the printer, complete Exercise 3D using the template file, as you did for Exercise 3C. Otherwise, open **Memotemp**, the file you saved in Unit 1. Print out a copy. Measure the depth of the pre-printed memo heading from the top of the page to the bottom of the heading text and allow for

2 or 3 clear line spaces after it. In total, this should be approximately 6.35 cm ($2\frac{1}{2}$ in). You are going to print Exercise 3D directly onto this pre-printed form in step 3.16.

3.13 Close the file **Memotemp**. Starting a new file, key in the following memo, using the line spacing shown.

From: Steven Murgatroyd, Assistant Premises Officer
To: Deborah Pickles, Training Manager
Ref: PP/33RT

REFURBISHMENT of the new training unit. (CAPS)

With regard to yr recent memo concerning the above, please find attached my estimate for complete refurbishment of the new unit, inclusive of decorations, furniture and misc items. Altho' (Altho') you did not specifically (requests) it, I have also included the approx cost of additional technology requirements such as telephone lines, computer cabling and (acsess) points etc.

There are several different ranges of furniture within the price bracket listed. (the) final choice is largely a matter of personal preference and I enclose several cats for you to look (thro'). (Aparently), no major structural alterations are necy (altho') I would (reccomend) that any (financiall) savings in this area be re-allocated to improving the cloakroom facilities (nearby). [I have invited several decorating contractors to meet with (you;) In particular I can (reccomend) a firm called Décor-8 who have previously undertaken work for us of a high standard. (There) contact name is (please insert contact name from Ex 3A).

A list of alternative dates is appended. (if) these are at all (inconveneint) I would (apreciate) it if you could notify

---

3.14 Following the instructions given previously, alter the top margin so that the body of the document does not 'overprint' on top of the pre-printed memo heading. Remember, you will probably need to enter a setting of approximately 6.35 cm ($2\frac{1}{2}$ in) for the top margin in order to allow for several clear line spaces after the letter heading text.

3.15 Save your document using filename **EX3D**.

3.16 Insert the pre-printed letterhead form (ie, the document **Memotemp** which you printed out at step 3.14) correctly into your printer. Print the document **EX3D** directly onto the pre-printed memohead form. Check your printout with the key at the back of the book. If you find any errors, retrieve the document and correct them.

3.17 Exit the program if you have finished working or continue straight on to the next unit.

By the end of Unit 4, you should have revised and practised all the techniques and skills needed for the RSA Text Processing Stage II Part 1 Award.

Look at your Progress Review Checklist and at your completed exercises to remind yourself of what you have learnt so far and to identify any weaknesses. Then complete the following exercises as revision.

 Exercise 4A ▶

4.1 Retrieve your letterhead template and key in the following text. Use either a ragged or justified right margin.

Our ref: TR/437/PN
Your ref: 1791/32BR

Mark the letter:
For the attention of
Abdul Aziz

Mace Brothers Ltd
Leverton Bussines Pk
SHIPLEY
SH4 9TW

Dr Sirs

As one of our most valued (cliants), I (were) very pleased
        you are
to hear that several members of staff from yr org
will be able to attend our Special Promotions event
next month.
    ◯ I attach a (maps) showing directions of how to get to
    (to) the venue and also an agenda for the afternoon.

There will be an opp to (disscuss) (any special) requirements you may have with the personnel (responsable) for each specialist area of work. In particular, I (beleive) you will be interested in meeting staff from our (Foriegn) Affairs depart_ment who have significant (experiance) in developing opps for |trade |and |overseas export. (may) I also (recomend) our Marketing Director, David Jamieson, who has assisted your co on a number of previous (occasion). David has developed some new methods of producing eye-catching (advertisments) that could be of benefit to yr own future publicity campaigns

(that you spend some time with)

yrs ffly
Terence Irvine /GENERAL MANAGER

4.2   Save your document using the filename **EX4A** and print one copy.

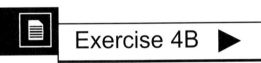

Exercise 4B ▶

4.3   Retrieve your memorandum template file and key in the following text. Use either a ragged or justified right margin. Save as **EX4B** .

From: Terence Irvine, General Manager
To: (please insert name of Marketing Director from Exercise 4A) , Marketing Director
Ref: TI/396

SPECIAL PROMOTIONS EVENT

With ref to the above event to be held next month, I have (circulate) letters to some of our major (cliants) who may be interested in attending. [I recall that you have previously done some work ~~with~~ with one co in particular, namely (please insert name of the company written to in Exercise 4A), and wonder if you could follow up my letter with a personal call.

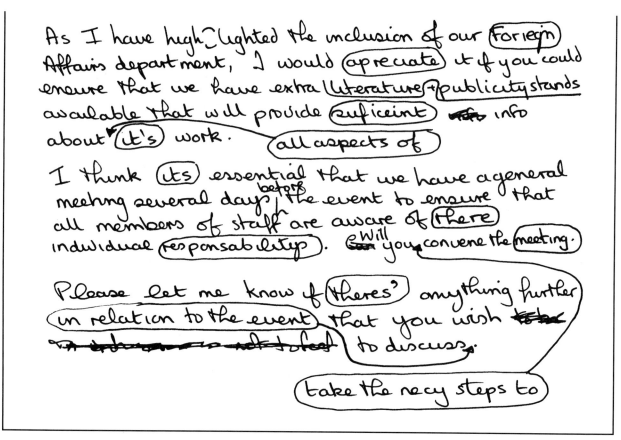

As I have high-lighted the inclusion of our (Foriegn) Affairs department, I would (apreciate) it if you could ensure that we have extra literature & publicity stands available that will provide (suficeint) ~~the~~ info about (it's) work. (all aspects of)

I think (its) essential that we have a general meeting several days before the event to ensure that all members of staff are aware of (there) individual (responsability). (Can) Will you convene the (meeting).

Please let me know if (theres') anything further in relation to the event that you wish ~~to be~~ ~~if there is not to feel~~ to discuss. (take the necy steps to)

4.4 Save your document and print one copy

📄 ## Exercise 4C ▶

4.5 Key in the following document using single line spacing except where indicated and following all the amendments shown. Use a justified right margin.

OUR FUTURE ON THE WORLD WIDE WEB

It is said that the Internet is one of the most significant (devellopments) of our time.

Net stretches around the globe like an electronic spider's web,

The ~~electronic Web stretches around the globe like an underground network,~~

interweaving communication links so that people from all parts of the (worlds) connect

computerised

in one massive ~~electronic~~ society.

Already, Internet telephones are hot products in the market place. Some feel that privacy and disconnection will become two of the most treasured qualities ~~conditions~~ of the 21st century. Analysts have theorised about the future implications of the Internet. People will expect to be connected to the Net wherever they are — on a plane, in a car, on a bicycle or in their living rooms.

The speed at which the Net is developing is faster than any technological change ever seen before.

Net Opinions

There are currently two main schools of extreme opinion about the wider impacts of the Internet on society.

operator: insert extra section here

Occupying the middle ground are those who understand the issues but believe thatt the 'worst-case' scenarios are unlikely. Optimism arises from the belief that today's hype about the Superhighway will be tomorrow's understatement.

To the right their are politicians, regulators and govermnents who seek to control the Web. Censorship is a topic frequently highlighted by the media as they unveil the ever-increasing amount of 'porn' freely available on-line. Right-wingers often find themselves caught between the desire to had a high-tech infrastructure for their economies and the fear that an uncontrollable universal network might prove extre;mely subversive.

Net Growth

keep this section in double line spacing

It is envisaged that by the turn of the millennium there will be ~~over~~ approx half a billion users linked to the Net, including almost every buisness, org, government authority, school and individual professional or entrepreneur.

The Era of the World Wide Web

We are entering a new era in which our economies and social fabrics will be shaped

by the world's public and private data networks.

Althuogh it may be relatively easy to grasp the idea of connecting the worlds'

computers together over the telephone lines, it may be more difficult to fully realise

just how much our lives will change as a result of such a simple concept.

National economic boundaries, already blurred by the use of private financial dealing networks, will cease to exist in a few years and companies (and countries) large and small, will have to re-engineer the way they conduct their business. This presents a significant challenge for tomorrows' business managers.

4.6 Save your document using the filename EX4C and print one copy.

To the left there is the 'wired community' which views the Net as uncontrollable and advocates that this giant global network joining ordinary people cannot be restrained ~~or~~ managed by any State or corporation.

By ⟨its⟩ nature it is subversive and it will bring an end to many traditional notions of

Western-style economics such as taxation, national currencies and national borders. National frontiers will ⟨continued⟩ to shrink as we become inhabitants of the 'Virtual Society' or cyberspace. It also means an end to your concepts of intellectual ~~abilities to maintain~~ property copyright.

⟨ operator: emphasise the words 'wired community' with italic ⟩

► Examination
Practice 1

By the end of Unit 5, you should have completed a mock examination for the RSA Text Processing Stage II Part 1 Award.

 RSA Text Processing Stage II Part 1 ►

This examination assesses your ability to produce, from hand-written and type-written draft, a letter, a memorandum and a report or article. The award demonstrates that you have acquired intermediate level skills in word processing (or typewriting).

The examination lasts for $1\frac{1}{4}$ hours and you have to complete three documents. Printing is done outside this time.

Examinations are carried out in registered centres and are marked by RSA examiners. The centre will give you instructions regarding stationery.

Letters must be produced on letterheads (either pre-printed or a template). Memos may be produced on pre-printed forms, by keying in entry details or by using a template. An additional piece of paper containing text to be incorporated into one of the documents will be handed to you during the examination.

Examination hints

When sitting your examination:

► you may use a manual prepared by the centre or the software manufacturer
► put your name, centre number and document number on each document
► check your work very carefully before printing – proofread, spellcheck; and
► assemble your printouts in the correct order at the end of the examination.

You are now ready to try a mock examination for Text Processing Stage II Part 1. Take care and good luck!

The list of assessment criteria for this examination is long and detailed. To be sure that you have reached the required standard to be entered for an examination, you need to work through several past papers and have these 'marked' by a tutor or assessor who is qualified and experienced in this field.

Results

► If your finished work has 4 faults or fewer, you will be awarded a distinction.
► If your finished work has between 5 and 11 faults, you will be awarded a pass.
► Results are sent to the centre where you sit your examination.

Retrieve your letterhead template and key in the following text. Use either a ragged or justified right margin.
Save the document as **EX5A** and print one copy.

Please mark the letter:
PERSONAL

Mrs Sarah Phelps
63 The Poplars
Kirkbride Cres
SKIPTON
BD25 1PB

You may return this to us, complete with yr sig, in the envelope provided.

Dr Mrs Phelps

With ref to yr recent enquiry ~~regarding~~ about poss vacancies in our Sales Department, please find enclosed an application form on which you may provided us with the info we need in order to assess ~~the~~ yr suitability ~~and~~ experience + for such a post.

Please note that we will require at least two refs, one of which should be from yr previous employer. If you wish, you may also include an up-to-date C.V. with the application form;

Altho' we do not have any immed vacancies, I beleive there will be an opp to apply for several positions in approx three month's time.

In the meantime, our Sales Manager, Mr Mila Yokovic, has informed me that he is considering the possibility of recruiting for a temp post in the interim period. I have passed yr details to Mr Yokovic so that he can contact you direct. Thank you for your interest in our co.

yrs scly
Gabrielle Macpherson
PERSONNEL MANAGER

Retrieve your memorandum file and key in the following text. Use either a ragged or justified right margin. Save the document as **EX5B** and print one copy.

FROM: Gabrielle Macpherson, ← *please insert*
TO: Mila Yokovic, ← *job titles from*
REF: GM/382 *Exercise 5A*

As (disscused) with you on the telephone earlier, I have (recieved) an enquiry in relation to poss vacancies in the Sales Department. I have (advise) the applicant of the likelihood of the forth coming permanent vacancies and also the temporary vacancy for which you were going to place an (advertisment).

I (reccomend) that you contact the applicant direct in regard to the latter vacancy. As she is quite (experianced) in sales I (beleive) you may be interested in meeting her.

The (applicants) name is Mrs Sarah Phelps. Her address is (please insert address from Exercise 5A). I have already forwarded the ~~sey~~ necy (correspondance) to her for completion. Can you let me know the outcome? [Apparently, I have not yet been provided with the criteria↓ I (apreciate) yr heavy workload at this time of the year but I am sure you will agree it is necy for you to provide ~~add~~ (suficeint) info to ensure that the job descriptions are relevant to yr ~~current~~ needs. ✓

(for the new sales positions.)

Document 3 ▶

Key in the following document using single line spacing except where indicated and following all the amendments shown. Use a ragged right margin. Save the document using the filename **EX5C** and print one copy.

(number the pages)

UNDERSTANDING ORGANISATIONS THROUGH METAPHORS

THE USE OF METAPHORS

(this paragraph only in double line spacing)

Metaphors are used essentially as a way of implying a hidden meaning through the use of words, or a figure of speech, which conjure up a particular image in the mind. Our thoughts are generally communicated to others *thro'* the language of written or spoken words. It has been said that a man's language is an index of his mind. Thus, the manner in which language is used can be seen as a mirror of the thought-processes that initiated it.

THE NOTION OF METAPHORS

(operator: insert extra section here)

To illustrate, extreme chauvinists have *beeen* quoted as saying that 'women have butterfly minds' - the implication here is that women lack *suficeint* concentration to produce effective results and the metaphor is used to personify a negative quality in women. In *a* similar context, but using a different metaphor, it has been ~~commented~~ *said* that 'men use helicopter planning procedures'. Although both figures of speech convey a similar concept of 'flitting from one thing to another', the choice of metaphor alludes to a quite distinct, and opposite, meaning.

The metaphorical play on words to allege a particular *ideas* or concept can even be applied in *a* different context *to the same word used*. Take, for instance, the word 'giant'. When we describe a certain individual as being like a gentle giant the metaphorical description implies a kind of clumsy docility. On the other hand, when Armstrong walked on the moon's surface, it was said that this was a giant step for mankind. *In the latter example, the metaphorical use of the same key word, giant, implies heroism and victory.*

METAPHORS AND ORGANISATIONS

Theorists often argue that many of our ideas about ~~firms~~ *orgs* are metaphorical, with a number of common images being used to demonstrate resemblance.

Managers who see ~~firms~~ _orgs_ as MACHINES often lose sight of the human factors, organising situations in a more mechanistic way with people making up the (inter;locking) parts of the machine to keep it functioning as a whole. The expression 'I feel just like a spare part' is, perhaps, an expression which may be heard when the organisational culture places greater emphasis on the smooth running of the mechanism than the needs of the operatives.

Organisations are ~~viewed as~~ _sometimes refd to as if they were_ ORGANISMS which can be born, grow, develop, or die as if somehow the organisation is a living thing able to respond and adapt to a changing environment and (develope)(it's) own evolutionary pattern.

Some managers see organisations as BRAINS. Phrases such as 'learning organisation' and 'brainchild of' draw attention to _info processing,_ learning and intelligence. It is as if the organisation can analyse situations, learn from its mistakes and reason on the way forward. [The key factor in the _effective_ use of metaphors is to build on them, to deliberately adopt a number of alternative viewpoints that may reflect organisational life. Developing such a multi-faceted approach will provide a broader focus for improving strategic decisions.

Conceptualisation is coloured in the way in which a metaphor is applied. _use bold and centring to emphasise this sentence_

Reading orgs through metaphors focuses attention on different aspects and general principles of organisational structure and behaviour – the way org interacts with its environment, views its workforce, operates decision making, defines strategies, distributes power, selects and promotes its management, and controls (or not) its management hierarchy.

📄 Additional text for Document 3 ▶

The use of linguistic metaphors draws attention to specific resemblance between different situations or (experiances) in order to highlight distinctive similarities. Take, for instance, the expression 'My head is like a spinning top!' By using a familiar figure of speech the speaker (are) able to personify the hidden state of mind he/she is feeling.

The particular metaphor singled out for use, however, can be used to force a particular viewpoint to the ~~fore~~ and push other viewpoints to the rear (if not concealing them altogether). (front)

unit 6

▶ Advanced multi-page documents

By the end of Unit 6, you should have revised previously-learnt text-processing skills such as:

▶ changing the typing line length
▶ indenting text
▶ insetting margins
▶ re-arranging text
▶ finding and replacing text.

In addition, you should also have learnt how to:

▶ insert headers and footers to appear on each page of a multi-page document
▶ allocate space within a document
▶ sort items, paragraphs or lists of information into a specific order.

Change the typing line length, indent and inset margins ▶

Please refer to Unit 1 of this book to refresh your memory on the methods for carrying out the above operations.

Exercise 6A ▶

6.1 Open the document you saved as **EX2B**. Save as **EX6A** and make the following amendments.

▶ Change the typing line length for the whole document to 13 cm (approx 5 in).
Note: In RSA examinations, it is not necessary for left and right margins to be equal although this does give a balanced appearance to a document. It is acceptable to change the typing line length by changing only the left or right margin. However, in practice, you will be governed by a number of factors, eg house style, author's preference, whether it is to be inserted into a binder, etc.

▶ Change the right margin format for the whole document to ragged (unjustified).

▶ Indent the whole section headed **Terms** by 4 cm (approx $1\frac{1}{2}$ in) at the right to allow for the later insertion of a graphic.

▶ Indent the left and right margins of the whole section headed **By telephone** by 2.54 cm (1 in).

6.2 Using the Print Preview facility, check the format of the document carefully, comparing it with the printout check at the back of the book. If you find any discrepancies, correct them. Resave your work and print one copy.

 # Rearrange text in a document

One of the most useful facilities of word processing is the ability to rearrange text on the screen and then print out when all the changes have been made. The first draft is then sent to the author who marks up the printout to show what changes are needed. The word processor operator can recall the document from disk, edit the text on screen and then print out the final copy.

Look back at Unit 2 to refresh your memory on correction signs.

Rearrangement of a document involves selecting, moving and copying blocks of text. Rearrangment of a document may involve the deletion of blocks of text, with or without replacement text being inserted. Rearrangement of a document frequently involves moving blocks of text from one position to another.

Rearrangement of a document can involve copying text, ie reproducing a block of text in another position within the document.

Note: Take care when following instructions not to confuse **move** and **copy**.

Read the following sections to learn quick and efficient methods of selecting, deleting, moving and copying text.

 # Select text

When you want to change a block of text in some way, it is necessary first of all to shade or highlight the particular section of text. In Word 97, this is called **selecting text**. The selected text shows in reverse – white letters on a black background, eg `selected text`.

To select	Keyboard	Mouse
One character (or more)	Press: **Shift + →** or **Shift + ←** Repeat until all required text is selected	Click and drag: The mouse pointer across the text
One word	Position the pointer: At the beginning of the word	Double-click: The word

Press: **Shift** + **Ctrl** + →, *or*
Position the pointer: At the
end of the word
Press: **Shift** + **Ctrl** + ←

To the end of the line	Press: **Shift** + **End**	Click and drag: The mouse pointer right or down
To the beginning of the line	Press: **Shift** + **Home**	Click and drag: The mouse pointer left or up
A full line	Position the pointer: At the beginning of the line Press: **Shift** + **End**, *or* Position the pointer: At the end of the line Press: **Shift** + **Home**	Click: In the selection border (left margin) next to the required line
A paragraph	——	Double-click: In the selection border, *or* Triple-click: Within the paragraph
The whole document	Press: **Ctrl** + **A**	Triple-click: In the selection border
Any block of text	——	Position the pointer: At the beginning of the text Hold down: The **Shift** key Click: At the end of the text (still holding down the Shift key)

To remove selection:
Click: In any white space within the document screen

 Delete a block of text ▶

To delete larger portions of text you select the block of text you wish to delete and then operate the
commands for deletion.

Keyboard

▶ Select: The text to be deleted (as
previously described in 'Selecting text')
▶ Press: **Del(ete)**, *or*
▶ Press: ← **(backspace/delete key)**

Mouse

▶ Select: The **Cut** button on the Standard Tool
Bar, *or*
▶ Select: **Cut** on the **Edit** menu, *or*
▶ Click: The right mouse button; select: **Cut**

Quick delete and insert text

To delete an incorrect section of text (of any size) and replace it with the correct text (of any size), simply select the incorrect text and key in the new text.

▶ Select: The text to be deleted (as previously described in 'Selecting text')
▶ Key in: The new text (without moving the cursor)

The incorrect text which was initially selected will disappear

 Restore deleted text (undo)

You can restore text which has been deleted accidentally. It is important that the pointer is in the correct place before you begin.

To restore text immediately after deleting:

Keyboard	Mouse
Press: **Ctrl + Z**	Select: **Edit** from the menu bar
	Select: **Undo Clear**, *or*
	Click: The ↶ **Undo** button on the Standard Tool Bar

Word 97 allows you to 'undo' many previous actions. These can be accessed by clicking on the ▾ button to the right of the ↶ **Undo** button on the Standard Tool Bar.

 Move a block of text

You can move sections of text quickly without deleting and retyping. This facility is sometimes called **Cut and Paste**. Text to be moved is 'cut' and placed on the 'clipboard', and then 'pasted' into its new position.

Keyboard	Mouse
Select: The block of text to be moved	Select: The block of text to be moved
Press: **F2**	Select: **Edit** from the menu bar
Move: The pointer to the new position	Select: **Cut** (The text disappears from the screen and is put
Press: ↵ (**return/enter**)	on the clipboard)
OR	Move: The pointer to the new position
Select: The block of text to be moved	Select: **Edit** from the menu bar
Press: **Ctrl + X** (the text disappears	Select: **Paste** (The text reappears in its new position)
from the screen)	OR
Move: The pointer to the new position	Click: The ✂ **Cut** button on the Standard Tool Bar
Press: **Ctrl + V** (The text reappears in	Move: The pointer to the new position
its new position)	Click: The 📋 **Paste** button on the Standard Tool Bar

Keyboard	Mouse
	OR
	Click: The right mouse button
	Select: **Cut**
	Move: The pointer to the new position
	Hold down: **Ctrl**; *and*
	Click: The right mouse button; *or*
	Click: The right mouse button
	Select: **Paste**

 ## Copy a block of text

Copying a block of text means that the text remains in its original place in the document and a copy of the same text is inserted elsewhere. This facility is sometimes called **Copy and Paste** – a copy of the text to be 'copied' is placed on the 'clipboard' and then 'pasted' into its new position.

Keyboard	Mouse
Select: The block of text to be copied	Select: The block of text to be copied
Press: **Ctrl + C**	Select: **Edit** from the menu bar
Move: The pointer to the required position	Select: **Copy** (The text remains on the screen and a copy is put on the clipboard)
Press: **Ctrl + V**	Move: The pointer to the required position
	Select: **Edit** from the menu bar
	Select: **Paste** (A copy of the text appears in its required position)
	OR
	Click: The ▣ Copy button on the Standard Tool Bar
	Move: The pointer to the new position
	Click: The ▣ **Paste** button on the Standard Tool Bar
	OR
	Click: The right mouse button
	Select: **Copy**
	Move: The pointer to the new position
	Click: The right mouse button
	Select: **Paste**

 ## Exercise 6B

6.3 Open the document saved as **EX2E**. Save as **EX6B** and rearrange the text as shown on the next page.

Left-align heading ← **RENTINET**

<u>YOUR GATEWAY TO THE WORLD</u>

For just £14.00 (+ VAT) per month plus an initial payment of only £25.00 (+ VAT), you can be instantly connected to the rest of the world!

With over 30 million users world-wide, the Internet is growing at an unbelievable 12% per month. Realise the potential for your organisation!

Let us take all the worry out of your technological information and communications systems.

copy to end of document

<u>SETTING-UP PACKAGE</u> (£25.00 + VAT at 17.5 % = £ 29.38)

Sign-up registration charge
Set-up of Internet account
Configuration of computer and modem
Fully-licensed software

Save 10 % if you pay for 1 year in advance - £22.00 saving!

The RENTINET Centre is open for Setting-up from
9.00 am to 6.00 pm   Monday to Thursday
9.00 am to 8.00 pm   Friday to Saturday   *10am – 4pm Sun*

Just bring along your PC – we'll do the rest. *or James Hall*
(Booking advised – Tel: Matthiäs Schneider on 01234-1098765)

We realise you may not be able to leave the office – we'll come to you. FREE setting-up session within 8 mile radius. £15.00 fee for 9 to 15 miles radius

We realise you may need help – the RENTINET Centre will be your <u>local</u> advice point – always there when you need us.

Still teetering on the brink? Take the plunge. RENTINET is your guarantee of a safe landing!

<u>SYSTEM CHECK</u>

Your IBM-compatible PC will need:

Windows 3.1	4 Mb RAM	5 Mb free hard disk space
Windows 95	8 Mb RAM	20 Mb free hard disk space
Apple Macintosh	8 Mb RAM	5 Mb free hard disk space

6.4   Using the print preview facility, check the format of the document carefully. Do not close the file. Resave the document. There is no need to print at this stage.

6.5 Add the following text to the end of the document on your screen.

Whether you are a small bus user or you use a computer at home for study and general interest, we can offer you expert help. Our specialist technicians are well trained and they speak *your* language. We won't confuse you with unnecessary jargon — just tell us what you want from yr computer and we'll tell you how to get started. [Many of our recent customers, who were new to computer use, are now happily using E-mail to communicate with friends and colleagues for bus or pleasure. [Students of all ages can enjoy ~~access~~ use to an endless source of information in the form of text and graphics. [Business users can be sure that the info in their reports is up-to-date and relevant. [Anyone who has an (hobby or interest) can communicate with others of a like mind through a News group.

OPEN 7 DAYS — ALWAYS THERE WHEN YOU NEED US ⎱ (double spacing and bold)
WHY WAIT — JOIN THE INTERNET CROWD TODAY! ⎰

(Centre) ⟶ <u>RENTINET TEL 01234-1098765</u>

6.6 Proofread the additional text carefully. Remember to insert page numbering as the document now takes up more than one page. Do not close the file. Resave the document. There is no need to print at this stage.

 # Find (search) and replace ▶

In word processing, it is possible to automatically find a given word or phrase and exchange it for another given word throughout a document.

You can use Word 97's find and replace function in two different ways (the first method is the safer in examinations):

1 You can ask Word 97 to stop every time it has located the 'find' word and wait for your confirmation before it 'replaces' the word (Replace). If you find an entry that you do not wish to be changed, you can skip over it and move to the next occurrence of the search (Find Next).

2 You can allow Word 97 to go straight through the document 'finding and replacing' without stopping for confirmation from you (Replace All).

Keyboard	Mouse and menu
Press: **Ctrl + H**	Select: **Edit**, **Replace**

The Find and Replace dialogue box is displayed on screen.

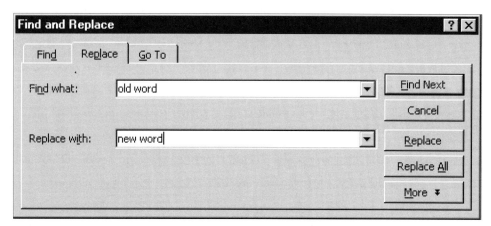

Figure 6.1 Find and Replace dialogue box

► Select: The **Find** tab
► In the **Find what** box, key in: The text to be searched for
► Select: The **Replace** tab
► In the **Replace with** box, key in: The replacement text
► Click: The **Find next** button

The **Go To** tab allows you to move to a specified place in the document.

Select from the Find & Replace dialogue buttons as appropriate

Button	Action
Find Next	Skips an entry which you do not wish to be changed and moves to the next occurrence of the search
Replace	Allows control over each replacement one at a time
Replace All	Replaces all occurrences automatically
More	Displays more advanced find and replace criteria. (**More** changes to **Less** when you select more advanced criteria.) This option includes:

	Match Case	Finds the exact combination of uppercase and lowercase letters
	Find whole words only	Finds occurrences that are not part of a larger word, (eg the word **rate** could appear in i**rate**, **crate**, desec**rate**d)
	Use wild cards	Searches for words using a **?** for variable characters, eg keying in **gr?y** in the **Find What** box and then clicking **Use wildcards** would find both **grey** and **gray** in the text.
	Sounds like	Searches for words which are pronounced like the **Find What** text, (eg your and you're)
	Find all word forms	Searches for words based on the same root word
	Format	Replaces text formatting, eg replace bold with underline
	Special	Finds special characters such as paragraph mark, graphic, etc
	Search	► **All** – searches through all of the document ► **Down** – searches from the cursor to the end of the document ► **Up** – searches from the cursor to the start of the document

Keyboard	Mouse and menu
Press: **Esc** to finish	Select: **Cancel** to finish

Note: Sometimes you can't see the text under the dialogue box so you can't decide whether to replace or not! Using the mouse, point to the middle of the horizontal blue bar running across the top of the dialogue box and drag the box down to the bottom left or right of screen.

 ## Find text (without replacing)

If you only want to find text (without replacing it) similar commands can be accessed through the **Find** dialogue box

Keyboard	Mouse and menu
Press: **Ctrl + F**	Select: **Edit**, **Find** from the menu

 ## Exercise 6B continued

6.7 Rentinet has decided to change its name. Use the Find/Replace function to change the name **Rentinet** to **Supernet** every time it occurs in the document on your screen.

6.8 Check your document carefully, comparing it with the printout check at the back of the book. If you find any errors, correct them. Print one copy and re-save your work.

 ## Headers and footers

A header is a piece of text in the form of a title, heading or reference which appears at the top of all pages of a multi-page document. A footer is the same kind of text appearing at the bottom of all pages. Headers and footers are printed within the top and bottom margins.

This word-processing function allows you to 'set' the headers and footers by keying in the text once only. The header or footer will then automatically appear on all pages. Headers and footers can be edited if the text or layout needs to be changed.

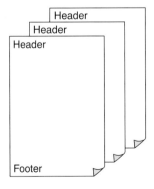

Figure 6.2

Using the header/footer function in intermediate examinations

In intermediate examinations, you will be asked to insert a header or a footer in to a two- or three-page document, and also to insert page numbering. Unfortunately, Word 97 does not allow you to omit the page number on the first page when using a header/footer. This is because page numbering operates within the header/footer text box. In RSA examinations, you will not be penalised for inserting a number on the first page. Therefore, we recommend that you insert the header or footer and accept page numbering on all pages. Otherwise, you would have to key in the header twice.

Although the benefit of using a header and footer in this way may not be apparent in a two-page document, if you were producing a document with many pages, the value of the header/footer command would be clear. You should practise using headers and footers so that you are familiar with the concept and would be able to use them in employment.

 # Set the format for headers and footers ▶

▶ Before keying in, *or*
▶ After keying in

Mouse and menu
▶ Position the cursor: At the beginning of the document
▶ Select: Header **and Footer** from the **View** menu

The Header text box and the Header and Footer Tool Bar are displayed on screen.

Figure 6.3 Header and Footer Tool Bar

To insert a text header:

▶ Key in: The required text in the **Header** text box
▶ Click: **OK**

Note: Header and Footer text can be formatted in the same way as document text – eg tab stops, text emphasis, font changes.

To insert a text footer:

▶ Click: The **Switch between Header and Footer** button on the Header and Footer Tool Bar
▶ Key in: The required text in the **Footer** text box
▶ Click: **OK**

The following options are available on the Header and Footer Tool Bar:

Tooltip title	Function
Insert Autotext	Inserts selected text into the header/footer, eg **Page 5 of 12, Last saved on...**

Insert Page Number	Adds the page number to the header/footer at the current insertion marker position
Insert Number of Pages	Inserts total number of pages in the document
Format Page Number	Allows page number format changes – eg Arabic, Roman etc
Same as Previous **Show Previous** **Show Next**	Used when creating different headers/footers for even/odd pages
Insert Date **Insert Time**	Automatically inserts the current details into the header/footer
Page Setup	Displays the **Page Setup** dialogue box – to allow changes to margins, layout etc
Show/Hide Document Text	Shows or hides the current document on the screen – a toggle switch
Close	Closes the Header and Footer Tool Bar and returns to the document screen

Note: Headers and footers show on the screen in Page Layout View and Print Preview only.

 # Delete headers, footers and page numbering

Mouse and menu

▶ Select: **Header and Footer** from the **View** menu
▶ Select: The header text, footer text or page number using the mouse
▶ Press: ← (backspace key) or **Del(ete)**
▶ Check: The deletion using Print Preview or Page Layout View

 ## Exercise 6C

6.9 Open the document you saved as EX6A. Save as **EX6C** and delete the page numbering already present. Set a header to show the following details:

Your name   **Exercise 6C**   **Your RSA Centre No** (if applicable)

If you have already typed these details at the top of Exercise 6A, delete them from the document – otherwise they will be printed twice!

6.10 Refer to the instructions on **page numbering** in Unit 2 and insert page numbers in Arabic format at the bottom left of each page.

6.11 Check that the header and page numbering are present on both pages of the document by selecting Page Layout View or by selecting File, Print Preview.

Note: If you find that headers and footers are not present in Print Preview, it may be necessary to increase the header/footer space allowance by changing the Page Setup as follows:

▶ Select: **File**, **Page Setup**.
▶ Increase the measurement in the **From edge** box (Header or Footer as appropriate).

6.12 Change the line length of the document to 15 cm (approx 6 in).

6.13 Reduce the indentation of the left and right margins of the section headed **By telephone** from 2.54 cm (1 in) to 1.27 cm ($\frac{1}{2}$ in).

6.14 Indent the section headed **Delivery** by 3.8 cm ($1\frac{1}{2}$ in) from the left margin.

6.15 Check your document carefully, comparing it with the printout check at the back of the book. If you find any errors, correct them. Save your work and print one copy.

 # Multi-page document – formatting requirements

In intermediate examinations, you will be expected to move around the document quickly, organise the editing of text and make the following formatting changes to multi-page documents:

▶ Allocate space
▶ Sort (re-arrange) items

Allocating space

You may be required to leave space within a document for the later insertion of a picture or diagram. In RSA examinations the measurement required is given in centimetres and in inches. The best time to insert the space is *after* all text insertion and amendments have been done but *before* pagination.

To leave a space of a given measurement (in, mm, cm or points) use the Format, Paragraph command:

▶ Delete: Any space already present
▶ Position the cursor: Just before the first character of the text that is going to come after the space
▶ Select: **Format**, **Paragraph**, **Indents and Spacing** from the menu bar
▶ Key in: The required measurement (in the stated unit of measurement) in the **Before** box

Word 97 will accept the measurement in centimetres, millimetres, inches or points, and will then convert this into the unit of measurement currently in use (usually centimetres).

 # Organise text in a multi-page document

When a document runs into several pages and there are many changes to be made, you may sometimes get a feeling of being 'lost' – particularly if you have been distracted. The following is a suggested method of working which you might like to adopt in order to avoid this:

1   Set the headers and page numbering and view them to ensure they are correct.
2   Carry out all the necessary text amendments, eg inserting or deleting of text throughout the whole document.
3   Move and copy blocks of text as requested throughout the whole document.
4   Find and replace text as requested.
5   Allocate space (using the given measurement) and indent or inset margins as requested.
6   Paginate your document as requested or as you think fit (read the instructions).
7   Spellcheck the whole document (use the Grammar Tool as well if necessary).
8   Proofread the whole document, comparing it word for word with the original.
9   Print Preview your document to make sure that it will be printed correctly.
10 Print your work.

 ## Move around the document – quick methods

When you are checking and proofreading a multi-page document, you need to be able to move quickly from one section to another. Practise the following quick cursor movements so that you become familiar with them and use them regularly:

To move:	Keyboard
Left word by word	Press: **Ctrl + ←** (arrow key)
Right word by word	Press: **Ctrl + →**
To the end of the line	Press: **End**
To the start of the line	Press: **Home**
To the top of the paragraph	Press: **Ctrl + ↑**
To the bottom of the paragraph	Press: **Ctrl + ↓**
Up one screen	Press: **Page Up**
Down one screen	Press: **Page Down**
To the top of the document	Press: **Ctrl + Home**
To the bottom of the document	Press: **Ctrl + End**

 ## Go to command

Keyboard	Mouse
Press: **Ctrl + G** *or* **F7**	Select: **Edit, Go To**

The Go To dialogue box is displayed on screen.

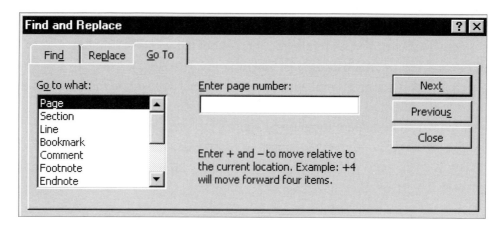

Figure 6.4 Go To dialogue box

Select from the options available as appropriate:

Go to – Go to what	Select: The type of location (eg page, line, field)
	Enter: The relevant number
	Note: (To go forward 2 pages, key in +2; to go back 4 pages, key in -4)
Previous and Next	Moves the cursor to the previous or next type of location described in **Go to what** box (eg page, line etc)
Find and Replace	Opens the **Find and Replace** dialogue box

  ## Sort (rearrange) items ▶

Rearrangement of a document often includes sorting a list of items into a given order. There are several ways to do this:

▶ Before keying in, use a piece of scrap paper to note down, in advance, the order in which the entries should be keyed in.
▶ After keying in, use the cut and paste functions to sort/rearrange the items into the required order.
▶ After keying in, use Word 97's automatic sort facility.

Word 97 will automatically rearrange information in selected rows, lists or in a series of paragraphs. The items may be sorted alphabetically, numerically or by date, and in either ascending (A-Z) or descending (Z-A) order. It is possible to sort an entire list, or to select a section of a list. If appropriate, you can sort a list before or after adding numbers to it – Word 97 automatically renumbers the list if the order changes.

If two items start with the same character, Word 97 takes account of subsequent characters in each item to determine the sort order. If an entire field is the same for two items, Word 97 takes account of subsequent specified fields to determine the sort order (eg surnames and first names).

▶ Select: The items or text to be sorted

▶ Select: **Sort Text** from the **Table** menu (if the items are in a table the command name changes to Sort)

The Sort Text dialogue box is displayed on screen.

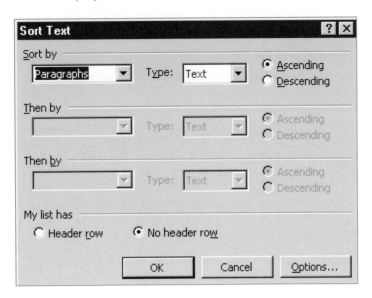

Figure 6.5 Sort Text dialogue box

Select from the sort options as appropriate:

Sort by	Select: **Paragraphs** or a **field number** – you can sort up to 3 fields or criteria
Then By	You may specify subsequent sort criteria for additional fields/columns by entering further sort criteria in the **Then By** boxes.
Type	Select: The type of information to be sorted – text, numbers or dates Word 97 will accept several different date formats (eg Jan 27 1995, 27 Jan 1995, Jan-95, 1-27-95, 1/27/95, 1-27-95)
Header Row/No Header Row	Select: The appropriate setting according to whether you wish the header row of your list to be included in the sort or not
Ascending	To sort in ascending order (eg A-Z, 1-100, 1 January 19xx – 31 December 19xx)
Descending	To sort in descending order (eg Z-A,100-1, 31 December 19xx – 1 January 19xx)
OK	Click: **OK** to operate the sort
Undo Sort	Click: The ↰ **Undo** button on the Standard Tool Bar

6.16 Open the document that you saved as **EX6C** if it is not already on the screen. Save the document as **EX6D** and carry out the following amendments:

> ▶ Change the position of the header to the top right of the document
> ▶ Change the position of the page numbering to the bottom right of the document
> ▶ Change the alignment of the document to the fully-justified style
> ▶ Rearrange the text as shown below.

<u>CUSTOMER INFORMATION</u>

Single line-spacing throughout whole document

PLACING ORDERS

It is our intention to achieve our target of supplying all of our customers with all of the goods ordered on the date promised. You can help us to help you by preparing your order before telephoning.

Copy to ✱

If you need further information on any of our products, we recommend that you refer to our company's Customer Information Service. We can give an immediate response to most queries. If necessary, we will check details with manufacturers and call you back within approximately 2 to 3 hours.

Move to ✱✱

<u>By telephone</u>

Ring our Order Hotline number when you have prepared a list of your requirements. Our operator will ask you for the following information: catalogue number, colour or size, description, quantity, price per unit, customer number.

If our lines are busy, you will be asked to leave your customer number and telephone number. We will call you back as soon as we possibly can. This means that you will not be wasting valuable time.

<u>By fax</u>

If you have access to a fax machine, we would be pleased to receive your order in this way to save you time and money. We supply order forms in the form of a printed pad to ensure no details are omitted. Please do remember to tell us if you require delivery to an address which is different to the one registered on our customer database and which is normally used for all correspondence.

If you need to contact us after office hours, 9.00 am to 5.30 pm Monday to Friday, our answerphone will record your message and/or your order.

Info Service ✱✱

Leave a space of 3.8 cm (1½") here please

Margins as for By telephone section when moved

<u>Terms</u>

Pre-paid by 1 week or cash on delivery. Bank or trade references will take about 10 days; after this clearance time we will accept cheques. Returned or re-presented cheques will be charged at £15 on each occasion.

We reserve the right not to accept orders, and all goods remain our property until they have been paid for.

Your signature on delivery acknowledges receipt of all the goods shown on the invoice at the price given and in good condition. Claims can be accepted only on concerns regarding quality. Contact the Customer Information Service in the unlikely event of such a problem. We will do our best to resolve the issue to your satisfaction.

<u>Delivery</u>

Refer to our map (on separate page at front of catalogue) to determine the day of the week when deliveries are made to your area. The minimum order amount is shown on this page. We feel sure you will appreciate that an order must be sufficiently large to justify **free delivery.**

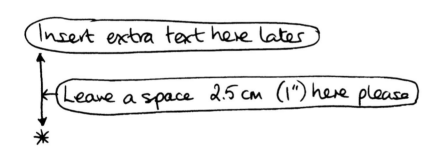

Insert extra text here later

Leave a space 2.5 cm (1") here please

6.17 Add the text shown on the next page, sorting the items into ascending alphabetical order and allocating space between paragraphs as requested.

Product Info

The following info is given in our cat & is displayed clearly in the warehouse for cash and carry clients:

Gluten-free products
Organically grown or produced products
Unit price
Vegan Products
Unit size
Warehouse location codes
Country of origin
Sugar-free products

6.18 Replace the word **Customer** with the word **Client** throughout the document wherever it occurs.

6.19 Proofread your work carefully. Using the print preview facility, check the format of the document carefully comparing it with the printout check at the back of the book. If you find any errors, correct them. Resave the document and print one copy.

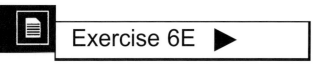

Exercise 6E ▶

6.20 Open the document that you saved as **EX6B**. Save it as **EX6E** and carry out the following amendments:

▶ Change the line length of the document to 13 cm.
▶ Change the alignment of the document to the fully-justified style.
▶ Insert a header
  Your name   Exercise 6E   Centre No (if applicable)
▶ Insert a footer: **Supernet Centre** using Times New Roman, font size 10, italic and centred.
▶ Delete the existing page numbering and insert page numbering at the top right of each page.
▶ Sort the list of items under the heading **Setting-up package** into ascending alphabetical order.

6.21 Using the print preview facility, check the format of the document carefully, comparing it with the printout check at the back of the book. If you find any errors, correct them. Resave the document and print one copy.

6.22 Exit the program if you have finished working or continue straight on to the next unit.

unit 7

▶ Tables

By the end of Unit 7, you should have learnt how to:

▶ complete a table with sub-divided columns and multi-line headings
▶ rearrange/sort items in the table into a specified order.

Tables ▶

Data is often presented in columns within letters, memos and reports in order to convey information quickly and clearly. Tabulated columns of information are also used for separate tables and accounts. Word 97 offers several different methods for producing a table, including the **Insert Table** and **Tables and Borders** facility. You should practise using both methods and choose the one you feel most comfortable with, although you can actually use a combination of both if you wish.

In the Stage II Part 2 examination you will be asked to key in a table with a number of columns containing a large amount of data, and which may include sub-divided or multi-line column headings. You will also be asked to sort the data in to a particular order. Instructions on the different methods of producing a table were included in the first book of this series but are repeated in this unit again for ease of reference.

If the table is quite large, you may also need to think about making it fit on the paper size which you are using (usually A4) by either reducing the left and right margins to 1.27cm ($\frac{1}{2}$ in) or reducing the font size. It is best to do this before the table is inserted. Although extra rows can be added quite easily, adding extra columns can create difficulties.

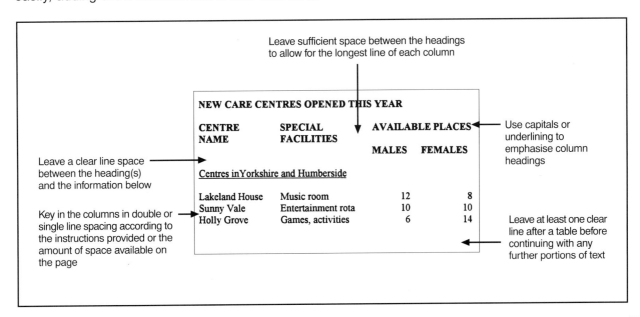

Leave sufficient space between the headings to allow for the longest line of each column

NEW CARE CENTRES OPENED THIS YEAR

CENTRE NAME	SPECIAL FACILITIES	AVAILABLE PLACES	
		MALES	FEMALES
Centres in Yorkshire and Humberside			
Lakeland House	Music room	12	8
Sunny Vale	Entertainment rota	10	10
Holly Grove	Games, activities	6	14

Use capitals or underlining to emphasise column headings

Leave a clear line space between the heading(s) and the information below

Key in the columns in double or single line spacing according to the instructions provided or the amount of space available on the page

Leave at least one clear line after a table before continuing with any further portions of text

Note: In the examination you will be asked to move a section of the table, such as a column, to a different place. If the table has sub-divided and/or multi-line column headings it is often more difficult to change the layout afterwords. It is suggested that you plan out the table layout on a piece of scrap paper beforehand. Spending a few minutes at the planning stage may save you a lot more time and frustration later!

 ## Insert table facility ▶

Mouse & Tool Bar method

▶ Position: The cursor where you want the table to be placed
▶ Click: The **Insert Table** button on the Standard Tool Bar
    A drop-down grid of rows and column cells appears on screen

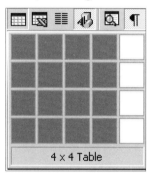

Figure 7.1 Insert Table drop-down grid

▶ Select: The number of rows and columns required by dragging the mouse pointer across the grid until thc bottom of thc grid displays the correct layout (eg 4 x 4 Table). The grid will increase in size as you drag the mouse.
▶ Release: The mouse button

Menu Method

▶ Position: The cursor where you want the table to be placed
▶ Select: **Insert Table** from the **Table** menu

The Insert Table dialogue box appears on screen.

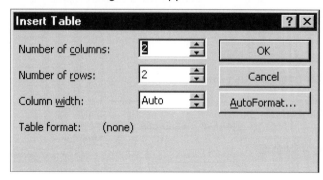

Figure 7.2 Insert Table dialogue box

Number of columns   Enter: The required number of vertical columns

Number of rows   Enter: The required number of horizontal rows

Column width (optional)	Accept: The default setting (Auto), *or* Select: A column width Click: **OK**
AutoFormat...	The **AutoFormat Table** dialogue box appears on screen
To remove borders or other formatting:	Select: From the special formatting options (the different effects available, eg borders, shading, 3D effects, can be seen in the **Preview** Box) Select: **(none)** from the **Formats** drop-down menu Click: **OK** when you have made your final choices

 ## Tables and borders facility ▶

Mouse & Tool Bar method

▶ Position the cursor: Where you want the table to be placed
▶ Click: The **Tables and Borders** button on the Standard Tool Bar

The Tables and Borders dialogue box appears on screen.

Figure 7.3 Tables and Borders dialogue box

Use the **✎ Draw Table** tool like a pen to draw your table layout directly on to the screen.

▶ Click and drag: To draw the table outline and the cell divisions inside the table

You can edit the table later to make individual cells any height and width you want.

Use the **✐ Eraser** tool to remove any cell, row, or column partition that you don't want, or to merge two adjacent cells vertically or horizontally.

Select: The entire table or the individual cells to which you wish to apply a border, or no border

Use: The **▦ ▾ Border styles** tool to set the table's ruled lines. You can choose to have no lines at all on the table by selecting the last option at the bottom right:

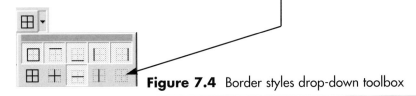

Figure 7.4 Border styles drop-down toolbox

To close the toolbox:
Click: The **⊞ Tables and Borders** button again

Move around ▶

Arrow keys   You can move around the table using the appropriate arrow keys

Tab   Moves right one cell (or inserts a new row when pressed in the last table cell)

Shift + **Tab**   Moves left one cell

Ctrl + **Tab**   Moves to the next tab stop in the cell

Alt + **Home** or **End**   Moves to the first or last cell in the same row

Alt + **PgUp** or **PgDn** Moves to the top or bottom cell in the column

OR

Click: The mouse pointer in the cell you want to move to

Change the column width ▶

Mouse	**Menu**
Select: The column(s) to be changed Point to: The dividing line between the selected column and the adjacent column (the pointer changes to a ⬌ double-headed arrow) Drag: The column-dividing line to the left or right to increase or decrease the column width as appropriate Release: The mouse button	Click: In the column(s) to be changed Select: **Table**, **Cell Height and Width**, **Column** *Either:* ▶ Enter: The appropriate measurement in the **Width of Column** box, *or* ▶ Select: **AutoFit** to automatically resize columns so the width is correct for the content ▶ Click: **OK** *Note:* You can also specify the amount of space between columns if required.

To make several columns or cells exactly the same width:

▶ Select: The columns or cells
▶ Select: **Distribute Columns Evenly** from the **Table** menu, *or*
▶ Click: The 🏛 **Distribute Columns Evenly** button in the Tables and Borders Tool Bar

Change the row height

Mouse

Select: The row(s) to be changed
Check: That you are in Page Layout View
Drag: The row-dividing line (on the vertical ruler) up or down to increase or decrease the row height as appropriate

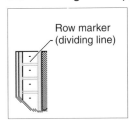 The pointer changes to a vertical double-headed arrow and the Adust Table Row tool tip appears

Release: The mouse button

Menu

Select: The row(s) to be changed
Select: **Table**, **Cell Height and Width**, **Row**
Specify: The appropriate row height measurement in the **Height of Rows** and **At (least)** boxes – Word allows you to enter the minimum or exact row height measurement in the **At** box
Select: The appropriate alignment in the **Alignment** section, ie **Left**, **Center** or **Right**
If row indentation is required, specify: How much to **Indent from left**
Click: **OK**
Note: You can also specify any **Row Alignment** and/or **Indent** if required

To make several rows or cells exactly the same height:

▶ Select: The rows or cells
▶ Select: **Distribute Rows Evenly** from the **Table** menu, *or*
▶ Click: The ⊞ **Distribute Rows Evenly** button on the Tables and Borders Tool Bar

 Insert columns and rows ▶

▶ Position the cursor: Immediately below the place where you wish to insert another column or row
▶ Select: **Select Row** or **Select Column** from the **Table** menu
▶ Select: **Insert Rows** or **Insert Columns** from the **Table** menu

OR

▶ Press: The right mouse button
▶ Select: **Insert Rows/Insert Columns**

OR

▶ Position the cursor in the table
▶ Click: The **Insert Rows** button on the Standard Tool Bar

Delete columns and rows

▶ Position the cursor: At the place where you wish to make the deletion
▶ Select: **Select Row** or **Select Column** from the **Table** menu
▶ Select: **Delete Rows/Delete Columns** from the **Table menu**, *or*
▶ Select: **Table, Delete Cells, Delete entire column** or **Delete entire row**, *or*
▶ Press: The right mouse button
▶ Select: **Delete Rows**

OR

▶ Select: The column to be deleted
▶ Press: The right mouse button
▶ Select: **Delete Columns**

Align text or data in a column or row

To improve the appearance and legibility of text in a table, you can align the text or data in each individual column or row in the normal way by selecting one of the Alignment buttons on the Formatting Tool Bar:

▶ Select: The column(s) or row(s) for which you want to set the alignment
▶ Click: The appropriate alignment button on the Formatting Tool Bar

Remove borders/lines

▶ Click: Anywhere inside the table
▶ Select: **Select Table** from the **Table** menu
▶ Click: The [⬚ ▾] **All Borders** button on the Formatting Tool Bar
▶ Select: The [⬚] **No lines/borders** option

Merge cells

Select the cells you wish to join together, then choose one of the following merge methods:

▶ Select: **Merge Cells** from the **Table** menu, *or*
▶ Click: The right mouse button; *and* select: **Merge Cells**, *or*
▶ Select: The [⊞] **Merge Cells** button from the Table and Borders Tool Bar

Split cells ▶

Select the cell(s) to be split, then choose one of the following split cells methods:

▶ Select: **Split Cells** from the **Table** menu, *or*
▶ Click: The right mouse button; *and* select: **Split Cells**, *or*
▶ Select: The **Split Cells** button from the Table and Borders Tool Bar

The Split Cells dialogue box appears on screen.

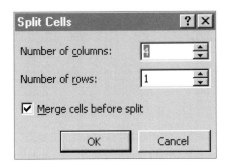

Figure 7.5 Split Cells dialogue box

▶ Enter: The number of columns or rows that you want to split the selected cell(s) into
▶ Click: **OK**

Sub-divided and multi-line column headings ▶

A multi-line column heading means that the column heading appears on more than one line. You can either allow the words to automatically 'wrap' on to the next line, or press the return key to key in a word on the next line down.

EVENT	START TIME	END TIME	ARENA
(col 1)	(col 2)	(col 3)	(col 4)

A sub-divided column heading means that the column heading may be divided into two or more subheadings. Follow the instructions given for merging and/or splitting cells to display the required layout

The table cells have been merged here to allow for the sub-divided column heading

EVENT	EVENT TIMES START END	ARENA
(col 1)	(col 2 + 3)	(col 4)

Exercise 7A – Practice exercise ▶

7.1 Use the **Insert Table** facility to create a table with 8 rows and 4 columns. Practise:

▶ moving around the table
▶ changing the column width and row height

- ▶ inserting a row and inserting a column
- ▶ deleting a row and deleting a column
- ▶ entering data in the table
- ▶ aligning data in each column to the left, right and centre
- ▶ merging and splitting table cells
- ▶ removing borders/lines from the table

Repeat the above using the 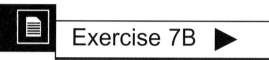 **Tables and Borders** facility.

7.2   Close the file without saving so that you are ready to start the next exercise with a clear screen.

Exercise 7B ▶

7.3   Starting with a new file, you are going to produce an unruled table with sub-divided and multi-line column headings. You can complete it using whichever method you prefer, and simply reproduce the table shown below (and skip step 7.4). However, if you need a bit more help, then you can follow the step-by-step instructions given in 7.4. As usual, use Times New Roman and font size 12.

You will need to refer back to the instructions for table layouts given earlier in this unit for **Insert table facility**, **align text or data in a column or row**, **merge cells**, **sub-divided columns**, **remove borders/lines**, etc.

NEW CARE CENTRES OPENED THIS YEAR

CENTRE NAME	SPECIAL FACILITIES	AVAILABLE PLACES	
		MALES	FEMALES
Centres in Yorkshire and Humberside			
Lakeland House	Music room	12	8
Sunny Vale	Entertainment rota	10	10
Holly Grove	Games, activities	6	14
Centres in Lancashire			
The Redway	Health, fitness club	16	14
Mountain View	Entertainment rota	15	15
Astonbury	All rooms en suite	8	10

> Align the data in the MALES and FEMALES columns to the right.
>
> Align the data in the CENTRE NAME and SPECIAL FACILITIES columns to the left.

Full details of the facilities at each Care Centre are available on request from Head Office. Cost of care varies between centres.

7.4   Follow these step-by-step instructions to reproduce the table layout shown in step 7.3. If you make a mistake as you are going along, use the ↶ **Undo** button to go back a step.

- ▶ Click: The Insert Table icon on the Standard Tool Bar and insert a table of 11 rows by 4 columns as shown below.

▶ Enter the data in each column and row as shown below.

CENTRE NAME	SPECIAL FACILITIES	AVAILABLE PLACES	
		MALES	FEMALES
Centres inYorkshire and the Humber			
Lakeland House	Music room	12	8
Sunny Vale	Entertainment rota	10	10
Holly Grove	Games, activities	6	14
Centres in Lancashire			
The Redway	Health, fitness club	16	14
Mountain View	Entertainment rota	15	15
Astonbury	All rooms en suite	8	10

Do not press ⏎ here

▶ Reduce the width of columns 3 and 4. Use the Merge Cells facility to merge the cells shown shaded in the table so that the layout appears as shown below.

CENTRE NAME	SPECIAL FACILITIES	AVAILABLE PLACES	
		MALES	FEMALES
Centres inYorkshire and the Humber			
Lakeland House	Music room	12	8
Sunny Vale	Entertainment rota	10	10
Holly Grove	Games, activities	6	14
Centres in Lancashire			
The Redway	Health, fitness club	16	14
Mountain View	Entertainment rota	15	15
Astonbury	All rooms en suite	8	10

You do not need to shade the cells yourself – the shading is simply to show you which cells are merged

▶ Insert a clear line space above and below the section headings where the arrows are shown below.

▶ Align the data in each section of the **MALES** column to the right.

▶ Align the data in each section of the **FEMALES** column to the right.

▶ Centre the data in the **AVAILABLE PLACES** cell.

CENTRE NAME	SPECIAL FACILITIES	AVAILABLE PLACES	
		MALES	FEMALES
Centres inYorkshire and the Humber			
Lakeland House	Music room	12	8
Sunny Vale	Entertainment rota	10	10
Holly Grove	Games, activities	6	14
Centres in Lancashire			
The Redway	Health, fitness club	16	14
Mountain View	Entertainment rota	15	15
Astonbury	All rooms en suite	8	10

▶ Key in the title for the table **NEW CARE CENTRES OPENED THIS YEAR**.

▶ Use the Select Table facility from the Table menu to select the entire table, then remove all table borders/lines.

▶ Key in the paragraph shown below the table **Full details of the facilities at each...**

NEW CARE CENTRES OPENED THIS YEAR

CENTRE NAME	SPECIAL FACILITIES	AVAILABLE PLACES	
		MALES	FEMALES

Centres in Yorkshire and Humberside

Lakeland House	Music room	12	8
Sunny Vale	Entertainment rota	10	10
Holly Grove	Games, activities	6	14

Centres in Lancashire

The Redway	Health, fitness club	16	14
Mountain View	Entertainment rota	15	15
Astonbury	All rooms en suite	8	10

Full details of the facilities at each Care Centre are available on request from Head Office. Cost of care varies between centres.

7.5 Click on each section and check that it is in the right font size (by checking Font Size on the Formatting Tool Bar). Save and print your document using the filename **EX7B**. Check your printout with the exercise above. If you find any errors, correct them on screen, save your document again and print again if necessary. Leave **EX7B** on screen so that you can practise the techniques of selecting and sorting items in a table.

 ## Select items ▶

Mouse or menu method

To select a single cell:

▶ Click: The left edge of the cell, *or*

▶ Place the mouse arrow: Anywhere in the cell

1	Red	Box
2	Blue	Tin
3	Pink	Bowl

To select a single row:

▶ Click: To the left of the row, *or*
▶ Select: **Select Row** from the **Table** menu

1	Red	Box
2	Blue	Tin
3	Pink	Bowl

To select a single column:

▶ Click: The column's top gridline or border when the black arrow appears, *or*
▶ Select: **Select Column** from the **Table** menu

1	Red	Box
2	Blue	Tin
3	Pink	Bowl

To select multiple cells, rows or columns:

▶ Drag the mouse pointer: Across the cells, rows, or columns, *or*
▶ Select: A single cell, row, or column
▶ Hold down: The **Shift** key, *and*
▶ Click: Another cell, row, or column

1	Red	Box
2	Blue	Tin
3	Pink	Bowl

To select an entire table:

▶ Select: **Select Table** from the **Table** menu

Keyboard method

To select the next cell's contents:

▶ Press: The **Tab** key

To select the preceding cell's contents:

▶ Press: **Shift + Tab**
▶ Hold down: The **Shift** key, *and*
▶ Press: An arrow key repeatedly

To select a column(s):

▶ Click: In the column's top or bottom cell
▶ Hold down: The **Shift** key, *and*
▶ Press: The ↑ **Up arrow** or ↓ **Down arrow** key repeatedly

To extend a selection (or block):

▶ Press: **Ctrl + Shift + F8**
▶ Press: The arrow keys to extend in the required direction
▶ Press: **Esc** to cancel selection mode

To remove the selection:

▶ Press: **Shift** + **F8**

▶ Press: **Esc** to cancel selection mode

To select an entire table:

▶ Press: **Alt** + **5** on the numeric keypad (with **Num Lock** off)

 ## Sort items

You can either sort the whole table or a specific selection of cells, rows or columns. For example:

B2	Red	Box
T7	Blue	Tin
B4	Pink	Bowl

◄— The table **before** sorting

T7	Blue	Tin
B4	Pink	Bowl
B2	Red	Box

◄— The table **after** sorting by **Column 2**, **Text**, and **Ascending** (items appear in alphabetical order of colour)

A) Mary's containers		
B2	Red	Box
T7	Blue	Tin
B4	Pink	Bowl
B) John's containers		
T8	Orange	Tube
B5	Green	Basket
C6	Brown	Can

◄— The table sections and rows **before** sorting

A) Mary's containers		
T7	Blue	Tin
B4	Pink	Bowl
B2	Red	Box
B) John's containers		
C6	Brown	Can
B5	Green	Basket
T8	Orange	Tube

◄— The table **after** sorting first the rows in section **A)** and then the rows in section **B)** by **Column 2**, **Text**, and **Ascending** (items appear in alphabetical order of colour by section)

Sorting items in a table

▶ Select: Either the whole table, or the specific rows and/or columns that you want to sort (see previous instructions on selecting items in a table)

▶ Select: **Sort** from the **Table** menu

The Sort dialogue box is displayed on screen.

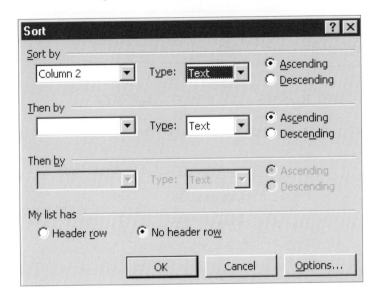

Figure 7.6 Sort dialogue box

Select from the sort dialogue options as appropriate (see Unit 6, p. 71).

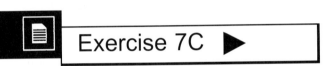

Exercise 7C ▶

7.6 If **EX7B** is no longer as you originally saved it, close the file without saving then retrieve the correct version and save it as **EX7C** before carrying out the following amendments:

▶ Move the **Centres In Yorkshire and the Humber** section so that it comes after the **Centres in Lancashire** section (using either the cut and paste or the drag and drop method).

Practise using the **Sort** facility:

▶ Sort the no of **FEMALES** within each section into exact ascending numerical order. Ensure all corresponding details are also moved.

▶ Sort the no of **MALES** within each section into exact descending numerical order. Ensure all corresponding details are also moved.

▶ Sort the **SPECIAL FACILITIES** within each section into exact alphabetical order. Ensure all corresponding details are also moved.

Complete a final sort:

▶ Sort the **CENTRE NAME** within each section into exact alphabetical order. Ensure all corresponding details are also moved.

7.7 Save your document and print one copy. Check your printout with the key at the back of the book. If you find any errors, correct them on screen, save and print your document again if necessary.

7.8 Starting with a new file, key in the following table. Save and print your document using the filename **EX7D**. Check your printout with the key at the back of the book. If you find any errors, correct them on screen and save and print your document again if necessary.

NEW PROPERTIES

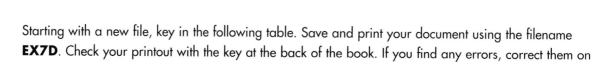

change the property areas in each section to all capital letters, eg DEVERTON

PROPERTY AREAS	NUMBER OF ROOMS		PRICE	GARAGE
	TOTAL	BEDROOMS		

Terraced Properties

Deverton	6	2	£58,000.00	N
Barwalk	9	4	£65,000.00	Y
Firth Bridge	3	1	£32,000.00	Y

Semi-detached Properties

Windy View	7	3	£48,000.00	N
Messeley	4	2	£65,000.00	N
Rook Lea	8	3	£82,000.00	Y

Detached Properties

Asterby	8	4	£98,000.00	Y
Penborough	11	5	£125,000.00	Y
Kingsway	8	3	£95,000.00	Y

The above properties are new on the market this week and therefore are not displayed in our current brochure. Full written details are available from the office receptionist but photographs may still be awaited.

Move the PRICE section to become the last section after GARAGE.

Move the Terraced Properties section so that it appears after the Detached Properties section

Sort into exact numerical order of PRICE starting with the cheapest in each section. Ensure that all corresponding details are also moved.

Align the columns as follows: PROPERTY AREAS to the left. PRICE and GARAGE to the right. TOTAL and BEDROOM centred.

DO NOT RULE

Exercise 7E ▶

7.9 Starting with a new file, key in the following table. Save and print your document using the filename **EX7E**. Check your printout with the key at the back of the book. If you find any errors, correct them on screen and save and print your document again if necessary.

(underline + bold this line)

Log of technician call-outs by time period over the last year

UNIT CALL-OUTS	AVERAGE VISIT TIME	NUMBER OF RECORDED VISITS	
		JANUARY TO JUNE	AUGUST TO DECEMBER
Acting Technician: Barry Stevens			
Marketing Unit	1 hr 10 mins	3	7
Personnel Unit	35 mins	7	4
Finance Unit	55 mins	5	5
Acting Technician: Herman Van Der Gouw			
Stores Unit	30 mins	2	4
Sales Unit	1hr 20 mins	8	12
Purchasing Unit	50 mins	6	7
Acting Technician: Dianne Weston			
Executive Unit	1 hr 15 mins	6	4
Export Unit	45 mins	3	5
Clerical Unit	15 mins	15	17

DO NOT RULE

(you may retain the abbreviations hr and mins)

The log has identified a significant trend for increased technician visits during the second half of the yr. The visit time spent in each unit shows a marked variance and further analysis will be conducted to ascertain the reasons behind this.

Please move the AVERAGE VISIT TIME section to become the last column after the NUMBER OF RECORDED VISITS section.
Also move the Herman Van Der Gouw section after the Dianne Weston section.

Sort into exact alphabetical order of UNIT within each section. Ensure that all the corresponding details are also moved.

unit 8

> ## ▶ Standard paragraphs

By the end of Unit 8, you should have learnt how to:

▶ create standard paragraphs, phrases or portions of text which may be used frequently

▶ retrieve and insert standard paragraphs, phrases or portions of text into a document as required.

 ## Standard paragraphs (boilerplating)

Many letters or documents have some parts in them that are identical in content. This can mean keying in the same portions of text over and over again, eg company addresses, standard paragraphs or the salutation at the end. In Word 97 you can store text or graphics that you use repeatedly and insert them as required into any document. This can obviously save you a great deal of keying-in time. This process is sometimes referred to as 'boilerplating'.

The method of saving standard paragraphs is exactly the same as saving any other document file. Using normal save procedures, you will be able to insert them into your main document as required. If you are inserting items that have been saved previously by someone else, you will need to identify the filename under which they have been stored. Often, a unique directory or folder is created to store standard paragraphs so that they can be easily retrieved.

Organisations often store a combination of standard paragraphs, phrases, portions of text and graphics in order to generate standard letters quickly. Retrieving pre-stored paragraphs at relevant points allows operators to compose standard letters very quickly. Standard letters need to be well displayed. Your layout, line spacing and heading styles should be consistent. You may need to emphasise text (bold, underline etc), extract information from another task and also route copies.

Don't forget to insert the date in the correct position on letters and memos.

 ## Standard paragraphs – document files

To create the standard paragraph file:

▶ Key in: The portion of text to be saved as a standard paragraph file

Save as a document file in the usual way:

▶ Select: **Save As** from the **File** menu
▶ Key in: An appropriate filename.
Note: If you use easily identifiable filenames, it will help you to retrieve the correct file. For example, **ENQUIRY** for a standard paragraph relating to customer enquiries.

To insert the standard paragraph file into your document:

▶ Position the cursor: At the place where you want the standard paragraph file to be inserted
▶ Select: **File** from the **Insert** menu
▶ Check: That the correct directory/folder is displayed in the **Look in** box

Then retrieve the standard paragraph:

▶ Select: The document file that you wish to insert
▶ Click: **OK**

8.1 You are going to create some standard paragraphs that may be useful for inserting into standard letters. Starting a new file, key in the following standard paragraph entry:

One of our sales advisers would be pleased to visit you, at a mutually convenient time, in order to discuss your particular requirements more fully. This is a completely free service offered by our company.

8.2 Save the standard paragraph under the filename **FREE**. Close the file.

8.3 Starting a new file for each standard paragraph entry, and with a clear screen, key in each portion of text shown in the left hand column below. Save each file separately using the filename indicated in the right hand column. Remember to close each file and start with a clear screen before creating and saving the next standard paragraph entry.

TEXT FOR EACH NEW STANDARD PARAGRAPH FILE	FILENAME
Thank you for your letter which we received	THANK
If you require any additional information please do not hesitate to contact us again.	INFO
Thank you for your recent enquiry regarding our range of business services.	ENQUIRY
We pride ourselves on offering excellent value for money and reliable, quality services.	VALUE
Our company operates to IIP standards and has over 15 years' experience in developing world class business services.	SERVICE
Please find enclosed our latest catalogue and price list.	PRICE
Part of the company's fundamental philosophy is to match all aspects of our business with customer satisfaction.	CUSTOMER
All our systems come with a 12-month warranty for parts and labour, with the option to extend for a three or five year period.	WARRANTY

8.4 You are now going to create some standard paragraphs that may be useful for inserting into memos. Create and save each of the following standard paragraph entries, using the filenames indicated. Remember to close each file and start with a clear screen before creating and saving the next standard paragraph entry.

TEXT FOR EACH NEW STANDARD PARAGRAPH FILE	FILENAME
We have received your application for staff development/training in the area of	TRAINING
As part of our standard procedure, we require you to complete the green Staff Development Form SD3 along with the signature of your line manager. The form is in duplicate – please send the top copy to Personnel and retain one copy for yourself.	PROCEDURE
At the end of the training session, please complete and return the blue Staff Development Evaluation SD4. Guidance for completing the form is on the back of the SD4. It is essential that we receive feedback from all participants.	EVALUATION
I am pleased to confirm that a place has been reserved for you. If you are unable to attend on the date and times shown below, please notify Personnel immediately so that we can re-allocate the place to another member of staff.	CONFIRM

 Exercise 8A

8.5   Starting with a clear screen, retrieve the file **LETTERTEMP**. Save as **EX8A** before keying in the text below and retrieve each of the standard paragraph files as indicated.

Mr Barry Fields
J D Fields & Co Ltd
Devenedge Road
BRADFORD
BD17 4RW

Dear Mr Fields

Insert the paragraph stored as: **THANK** last week. Unfortunately, the person to whom you addressed the letter left the company several months ago, which is the reason for the delay in our reply.

However, I have now passed your letter to our Customer Care Department for them to respond to the issues you raise. Insert the paragraph stored as: **CUSTOMER**

I note from your letter that you have a number of queries regarding our customised business services. Insert the paragraph stored as: **FREE** If you would like to take advantage of this offer, please contact our Sales Department on Extension 153.

Insert the paragraph stored as: **INFO**

Yours sincerely

Melanie Parkes
ADMINISTRATION CLERK

8.6   Resave your document and print one copy. Check your printout with the key at the back of the book. If you find any errors, retrieve the document and correct them.

8.7   You will be able to practise retrieving and inserting the standard paragraphs you have created in the next unit. Exit the program if you have finished working or continue straight on to the next unit.

unit

9

► Routing business documents

By the end of Unit 9, you should have learnt how to:

- ► prepare business letters and memoranda
- ► print letters and memos on pre-printed letterheads
- ► locate information in another document and insert it into a current document
- ► indicate routing of copies on business documents
- ► enumerate items.

Business letter and memo layout

Refer back to Unit 3 to refresh your memory on the correct layout procedures for business letters and memoranda, and on using either a pre-printed letterhead/memohead or a template.

Locate information from another document

Refer back to Unit 3 to refresh your memory on locating information from another document to insert into the current document.

Route copies ►

It is normal practice for the sender to keep one copy of a letter or memo for reference. Additional copies may be required for other people and this is usually indicated at the foot of the document.

Instructions may appear as:

> *Top and 2 copies please.*
> *One file copy and one for*
> *Sue Thompson. Indicate routing.*

The routing indication is inserted at the bottom of the document (under any enclosure mark). For example:

Copy: Sue Thompson
        File

When all the copies of the document have been printed, it is normal practice to indicate the destination of each copy by ticking, underlining in coloured pen or highlighting.

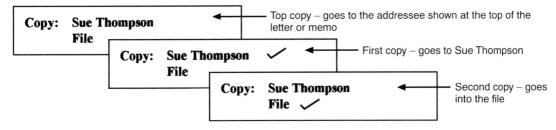

Copy: Sue Thompson
        File
— Top copy – goes to the addressee shown at the top of the letter or memo

Copy: Sue Thompson   ✓
        File
— First copy – goes to Sue Thompson

Copy: Sue Thompson
        File   ✓
— Second copy – goes into the file

Enumeration ▶

Word 97 can quickly create enumerated or bulleted paragraphs. Enumeration shows sequence while bullets emphasise separate items in a list. You can choose different styles of enumeration – capital letters, lower case letters, numbers or roman numerals, any of which can be followed by a bracket or a full stop or nothing. If you add, delete or reorder enumerated items, Word 97 will automatically update the sequence for you. It is usual to leave one clear space between enumerated items.

Bulleted list:	*Enumerated list - numbers*	*Enumerated list - letters*
• Apples • Oranges • Pears • Peaches	1) Wash and dry the fruit carefully. 2) Peel, remove pips and pith, then arrange in quarters.	a) Wash and dry the fruit carefully. b) Peel, remove pips and pith, then arrange in quarters.

Keyboard method

▶ Position the cursor: At the beginning of the paragraph to begin the enumeration
▶ Key in: The enumeration (eg A)
▶ Press: **Tab** to set the indent for the first line
▶ Press: **Ctrl + T** to set the 'wrap around' indent for all subsequent lines of the paragraph
▶ Key in: The rest of the text

Repeat the above for each enumerated paragraph.

Mouse and Formatting Tool Bar method

To create an enumerated list after typing:

▶ Select: The paragraphs or items to which you want to add enumeration
▶ Click: The ⊞ **Numbering** button on the Formatting Tool Bar

To create an enumerated list automatically as you type:

▶ Key in: **1)** followed by a space or a tab and the first paragraph of text

When you press ↵ (**return/enter**) to add the next paragraph or item, Word automatically inserts the next number.

Note: Type * instead of **1)** if you want to create a bulleted list.

To finish the list:

▶ Press ↵ (**return/enter**) twice, *or*
▶ Press: ← (**backspace**) to delete the last number in the list

Note: To alter the format of the enumeration follow the mouse and menu instructions below.

Mouse and menu

▶ Select: The paragraphs or items to which you want to add enumeration
▶ Select: **Bullets and Numbering** from the **Format** menu
▶ Select: The **Numbered** tab
▶ Click: The style you require from the visual display options given (a blue outline appears on the selected box)

▶ Select: **Customize** if you want to modify the style further, ie change the font, number style, indent, alignment, position, or number to start from

▶ Click: **OK**

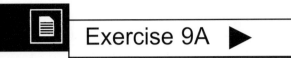

Exercise 9A ▶

9.1 Open the file **EX8A** and save as **EX9A**.

9.2 Delete the third paragraph.

9.3 Insert the following text and enumerated paragraphs after the second paragraph of the letter:

In particular we ~~are able to~~ offer:

a) Guaranteed delivery of any items ordered within 14 days from ~~initial to~~ initial order.

b) No ~~gats~~ quibble exchange or refund for unwanted (or) damaged goods within 28 days of purchase.

c) On²⁻⁰going support & advice [thro'] our Telephone Hotline.

9.4 Indicate the routing of the letter – one copy to Customer Care and one copy for the file.

9.5 Save the document and print one copy. Check your printout with the key at the back of the book. If you find any errors, retrieve the document and correct them.

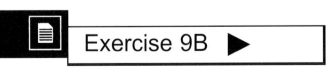

Exercise 9B ▶

9.6 Starting with a clear screen, retrieve the file saved as **Memotemp**. Save as **EX9B** and key in the text on the next page. Retrieve and insert the standard paragraphs where indicated.

FROM: Harriet Janson, Personnel Assistant
To: Kevin O'Flannagan, Purchasing Clerk
REF: GB/457

Staff development in health and safety ← (bold and caps)

(Insert the paragraph stored as: TRAINING) Health and Safety.

A copy of yr. application has been forwarded to yr. line manager, Paula Denny, for approval of your release from standard duties on one of the proposed training dates. Once this is confirmed we shall be able to reserve a definite place for you. In accordance with our standard procedures you will be required to undertake the following prior to the event:

1) Read the Health and Safety procedures and information in the booklet attached.

2) Complete the attached questionnaire based on your existing knowledge. You will need to take this with you to the training session.

3) Identify current Health and Safety work practices in your department and prepare an outline of where you think these may need to be improved.

(Insert the paragraph stored as: EVALUATION)

Thank you for your interest in this event.

(Use a justified right margin)

(Top and 2 copies please. One file copy and one for Paula Denny. Indicate routing.)

9.7   Save your document and print one copy. Check your printout with the key at the back of the book. If you find any errors, retrieve the document and correct them.

9.8 Starting with a clear screen, retrieve the file saved as **Lettertemp**. Save as **EX9C** and key in the text shown below. Retrieve and insert the standard paragraphs where indicated.

Our ref: VH/TS/564

Miss Tara Schmidt
14 New Ridgeway Rd
BRISTOL BS4 2TR

Top and 2 copies please.
One file copy and one
for Lee Johnson.
Indicate routing.

Dear Miss Schmidt

Insert the phrase stored as ENQUIRY

any aspect of
our business

Insert the phrase stored as VALUE   All our services can
be individually tailored to meet your specific needs.

Insert the phrase stored as SERVICE   We have a number
of Personal Consultants operating in your
area who would be pleased to review with you.

In relation to your enquiry about the purchase of
equipment (computer, we offer a specialist
range of state-of-the-art computers designed
to meet (business) needs. Insert the phrase stored as PRICE

Insert the phrase stored as WARRANTY

I will ask our Personal Consultant Manager,
Lee Johnson, to contact you as soon as poss in order to
(disscus) your requirements further.
Yrs sely
Vanessa Hartley
Business Development Manager

9.9 Save your document and print one copy. Check your printout with the key at the back of the book. If you find any errors, retrieve the document and correct them.

9.10 Exit the program if you have finished working or continue straight on to the next unit.

unit
10

▶ Consolidation 2

By the end of Unit 10, you should have revised and practised all the skills needed for the RSA Stage II Part 2 Word Processing award.

Exercise 10A ▶

Recall this document stored as **EX4C**. Save as **EX10A** and amend as shown below. Change to double line spacing (except where indicated) and use a ragged right margin. Adjust the line length to 12.5 cm (5 in). Save the document and print one copy.

OUR FUTURE ON THE WORLD WIDE WEB ← *bold and centre this heading*

It is said that the Internet is one of the most ~~significant~~ *amazing* developments of our time. //The Net stretches around the globe like an electronic spider's web, interweaving communication links so that people from ~~all parts of the world~~ *every extremity of the earth can* connect in one massive computerised society.

Analysts have theorised about the possible future implications of the Internet. People will expect to be connected to the Net wherever they are - on a plane, in a car, on a bicycle or in their living rooms. ~~Already, Internet telephones are hot products in the marketplace. Some feel that disconnection and privacy will become two of the most treasured qualities of the 21st century.~~

The speed at which the Net is developing is faster than any technological change ever seen before. *It demonstrates the reality of the theory of "increasing returns" - the more the Net grows, the more reason it has to grow.*

Net Opinions

There are currently two main schools of extreme opinion about the wider impacts of the Internet on society.

To the left there is the '*wired community*' which views the Net as uncontrollable and advocates that this giant global network joining ordinary people cannot be managed or restrained by any State or corporation.

By its nature it is subversive and it will bring an end to many traditional notions of Western-style economics such as taxation, national currencies and national borders. National frontiers will continue to shrink as we become inhabitants of the 'Virtual Society' or cyberspace. It also means an end to our concepts of intellectual property copyright.

move this section to the point marked Ⓐ

To the right there are politicians, regulators and governments who seek to control the Web. ~~Censorship is a topic frequently highlighted by the media as they unveil the over-increasing amount of 'porn' freely available on-line.~~ Right-wingers ~~often find themselves caught~~ *can be* *for* between the desire to have a high-tech infrastructure for their economies and the fear that an uncontrollable universal network might prove extremely subversive.

please put the words "increasing returns" in italic

Occupying the middle ground are those who understand the issues but believe that the 'worst-case' scenarios are unlikely. Optimism arises from the belief that today's hype about the Information Superhighway will be tomorrow's understatement. The ~~access~~ (access), ~~the~~ mobility and ~~the~~ ability to effect change are what will make the twenty-first century so different from the present.

Net Growth

It is envisaged that by the turn of the millennium there will be ~~approximately~~ over half a

billion users linked to the Net, ~~including almost every business, organisation,~~

~~government authority, school and individual professional or entrepreneur.~~

NET FUTURES
~~The Era of the World Wide Web~~

> copy this section to the point marked ✱

(We are entering a new era in which our economies and social fabrics will be shaped by the world's public and private data networks.)

Ⓐ

National economic boundaries, already blurred by the use of private financial dealing networks, will cease to exist in a few years and companies ~~(and countries) large and~~ ~~small,~~ will have to re-engineer the way they conduct their business. ~~This presents a~~ ~~significant challenge for tomorrow's business managers.~~ ◄

[Although it may be relatively easy to grasp the idea of connecting the world's computers together over the telephone lines, it may be more difficult to fully realise just how much our lives will change as a result of such a simple concept.]

insert this paragraph by 1.27cm (½") from both left and right margins and use single line spacing for this paragraph only.

This massive change will emanate from 3 events. Firstly, the proliferation of personal computers in the office and home and their integration with the telephone and television. Secondly, the cost of international phone calls (and data communications in general] will reduce drastically. 3rdly, there will be an almost global desire by governments to deregulate and privatise the telecommunications industry.

Operator
- insert SOCIETY ON THE NET to appear as a header on every page.
- apart from the main heading, change world to globe throughout this document.

Key in the following table. Save the document as **EX10B** and print one copy.

STAFF DEVELOPMENT EVENT - INTERNET TRAINING ← (bold)

DEPARTMENTAL ARRANGEMENTS		SESSIONAL ARRANGEMENTS	
EMPLOYEE POSITION	EMPLOYEE NAME	TRAINING SESSION DATE	TRAINING SESSION START TIME
Marketing and Sales Departments			
Marketing Officer	COOKE, V	7 October	10.30am
Sales Manager	YOKOVIC, M	23 October	9.30am
Sales Co-ordinator	ALLAN, F	7 October	10.30am
Marketing Director	JAMIESON, D	24 October	10.00am
Marketing Assistant	BROWN, L	23 October	9.30 am
Personnel and Central Administration Departments			
Administration Manager	FOGGERTY, N	24 October	10.00am
Personnel Assistant	O'MALLEY, B	7 October	10.30am
Personnel Manager	MACBETH, G	23 October	9.30am
Administration Co-ordinator	COOKE, R	23 October	9.30am
Personnel Assistant	JANSON, H	7 October	10.30am
Purchasing Department and Stores			
Stores Manager	SHARMA, Y	23 October	9.30 am
Assistant Stores Manager	MILTON, G	7 October	10.30am
Senior Purchasing Officer	BRADY, A	23 October	9.30 am
Transport Manager	BEDDOWS, J	24 October	10.00 am
Purchasing Manager	DENNY, P	7 October	10.30am

Internet Training Sessions for the staff named above will be held in Room C437. All staff are expected to attend on the dates and times stipulated.

Please sort TRAINING SESSION DATE into ascending date order within each section. Ensure corresponding details are also rearranged.

Please move EMPLOYEE NAME to be the first column

DO NOT RULE

Please move the Purchasing Department and Stores section to below the Marketing and Sales Departments

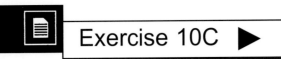
Key in the following document and insert the phrases as indicated. Save the document as **EX10C** and print one copy.

MEMORANDUM

FROM: Sam Byron, Computer Services Manager
TO: J Beddows, Transport Manager
REF: SB/JB/int56

INTERNET TRAINING

(Insert the phrase stored as: TRAINING) new technology. As part of the company's strategy to keep all staff up-to-date with information technology developments we are offering a number of training sessions on the Internet.

(Insert the phrase stored as: CONFIRM)

Please check date and time with Exercise 10B and amend if necessary.

J Beddows, Transport Manager: 22 October at 10.00 am.

(Insert the phrase stored as: PROCEDURE)

this line in bold

(Insert the phrase stored as: EVALUATION)

Other training events planned for this year are detailed below. I would be grateful if you could let me know which of these would be useful for you to attend.

a) Word 97 for Windows
b) Excel Spreadsheets
c) Video Conferencing
d) Access Database
e) E-mail (beginners and advanced)
f) PowerPoint
g) Microsoft Publisher

Top + 2 please. One for Personnel and one for our files. Indicate routing

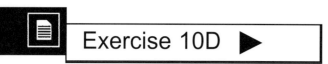

Recall this document stored as **EX10C**. Save as **EX10D** and amend as shown. Print one copy.

ACE BUSINESS SERVICES

MEMORANDUM

FROM: Sam Byron, Computer Services Manager
TO: ~~J Beddows, Transport Manager~~ G Milton, Stores Manager
REF: SB/JB/int56
DATE: today's

(bold and underline)

INTERNET TRAINING ◄

We have received your application for staff development/training in the area of new technology. ~~As part of the company's strategy to keep all staff up-to-date with information technology developments~~ We are offering a number of training sessions on the Internet.

I am pleased to confirm that a place has been reserved for you. If you are unable to attend on the date and times shown below, please notify Personnel immediately so that we can re-allocate the place to another member of staff.

G Milton, Stores Manager : 23 October at 9.30 am. ◄
~~J Beddows, Transport Manager: 24 October at 10.00 am.~~ *(bold+centre this line)*

As part of our standard procedure, we require you to complete the green Staff Development Form SD3 along with the signature of your line manager. The form is in duplicate – please send the top copy to Personnel and retain one copy for yourself.

At the end of the training session, please complete and return the blue Staff Development Evaluation SD4. Guidance for completing the form is on the back of the SD4. It is essential that we receive feedback from all participants.

↕ *(Leave at least 25mm (1") here)*

Other training events ~~planned~~ ~~for this year~~ are detailed below. ~~I would be grateful if you could~~ Please let me know which of these ~~would be useful for you~~ you would like to attend.

a) Word 97 for Windows
b) Excel Spreadsheets
c) Video Conferencing
d) Access Database
e) E-mail (beginners and advanced)
f) PowerPoint
g) Microsoft Publisher

(Please sort into exact alphabetical order)

(Use a justified right margin)

Copy: Personnel
       File

unit 11

▶ Examination Practice 2

By the end of Unit 11, you should have completed a mock examination for the RSA Stage II Part 2 Word Processing Award.

RSA Stage II Part 2 Word Processing ▶

This examination assesses your ability to produce documents such as: a notice; an article; lists of information; a table; and a standard document incorporating selected phrases, from handwritten and typewritten draft and from recalled text. The award demonstrates that you have acquired intermediate level skills in word processing.

The examination lasts for $1\frac{3}{4}$ hours and you must complete four documents, using a word processor. Printing is done outside this time.

Examinations are carried out in registered centres and are marked by RSA Examiners. The centre will give you instructions regarding stationery. Letters must be produced on letterheads (either pre-printed or a template) and memos may be produced on pre-printed forms, by keying-in entry details or by use of a template. The invigilator will give you instructions concerning the recalling of stored files.

Examination hints

When sitting your examination:

- ▶ you may use a manual prepared by the centre or the software manufacturer
- ▶ put your name, centre number and document number on each document
- ▶ check your work very carefully before printing – proofread, spellcheck
- ▶ assemble your printouts in the correct order at the end of the examination

You are now ready to try a mock examination for Word Processing Stage II Part 2. Take care and good luck!

The list of assessment criteria for this examination is long and detailed. To be sure that you have reached the required standard to be entered for an examination, you need to work through several past papers and have these 'marked' by a tutor or assessor who is qualified and experienced in this field.

Results

- ▶ If your finished work has 4 faults or fewer, you will be awarded a distinction.
- ▶ If your finished work has between 5 and 11 faults, you will be awarded a pass.
- ▶ Results are sent to the centre where you sit the examination.

Key in the following text and save as EX11A. No need to print a copy.

KIRKDALE SPA

The Guide is designed to help you and yr group to get as much enjoyment as poss from yr day out in Kirkdale Spa. [You will find a complete list of local attractions including the Waterfront, Cedar Abbey & the City Art Gallery. Contact names, telephone numbers, ~~and visiting times~~ opening hours and admission prices are given for each venue.

Many of our attractions offer special ~~rates~~ prices for groups. ✓ Please ~~contact~~ call the named official to receive help in ensuring an interesting and informative visit.

The Tourist Info Office for K— S— & district will be happy to help you to plan an interesting and successful day for yr group's visit. Simply telephone Susan Bywater on 01484-646/5636 with details of yr group numbers, ages, special interests etc.

The T— I— O— is open as follows:

| Mon – Fri | 9.30am – 5pm |
| Sat and Sun | 10.00 am to 6 pm |

Consider the following ~~options~~ alternatives:

City Art Gallery
Streamside Walk
The Waterfront
Maggie's Mill Shop

Cedar Abbey
Rowan Falls
Kirkdale Crafts

Please key in in one column at left margin

Preliminary Task 2 ▶

Key in the following blocks of text and save them under the filename shown. DO NOT PRINT.

I hope that you found the recent training day to be stimulating and relevant. As promised, I am writing to give further details of workshops which are scheduled to take place in the ~~Spring~~ Autumn.

Save as PHRASE11B

Students following programmes in leisure, tourism, outdoor recreation and business studies will assist in the research aspects under the direction of the College staff. We have agreed an action plan with those concerned.

Save as PHRASE11C

Meetings will be held on the first and third Tuesdays of each month commencing ~~an~~ in August. Please come along to the Elphin Room at the City Hall at 7.30 pm on Tuesday 6 August.

Save as PHRASE11D

Each group of students is to prepare and submit a report and presentation to the first workshop in September. Monthly meetings will be held to determine marketing strategies and identify resource needs so that promotional materials are ready for publication soon after Christmas.

Save as PHRASE11E

Recall the document stored as EX11A and save as UNIT11DOC1. Amend as shown, using double line spacing except where indicated. Adjust line length to either (a) 12.5 cm (5") or b) 50 characters. Use a justified right margin. Print one copy

Insert GROUP GUIDE as a header on every page

KIRKDALE SPA

Welcome to the comprehensive group guide to Kirkdale Spa.

Copy to ※

The Guide is designed to help you and your group to get as much enjoyment as possible from your day out in Kirkdale Spa.

You will find a complete list of local attractions including The Waterfront, Cedar Abbey and the City Art Gallery. Contact names, telephone numbers, admission prices and opening hours are given for each venue. Many of our attractions offer special rates for groups. Please call the named official to ~~receive~~ get some help in ~~ensuring~~ creating an interesting and informative visit.

Single line spacing

The Tourist Information Office for Kirkdale Spa and district will be happy to help you to plan an interesting and successful day for your ~~group;~~s visit. Simply telephone Susan Bywater on 01484-646 5636 with details of your group numbers, ages, special interests etc. [A]

~~Consider the following alternatives~~:

~~City Art Gallery~~
~~Streamside Walk~~
~~The Waterfront~~
~~Maggie's Mill Shop~~
~~Cedar Abbey~~
~~Rowan Falls~~
~~Kirkdale Craf~~ts

Please change Kirkdale Spa to Kirkdale Pennine Spa wherever it occurs in the document

~~The Tourist Information Office is open as follows:~~

Monday – Friday   9.30 am – 5.00 pm
Saturday and Sunday   10.00 am – 6.00 pm

retain single spacing

The Services Section of the group guide gives details of local tourist info centres, regional railways, airports, & coach and bus operators. A well-developed public transport system puts Kirkdale Spa firmly on the map. Our very successful Park and Ride scheme has been in operation for two years now, and is used by thousands of tourists annually.

The City Hopper and City Guide mini-buses offer cheap and frequent transport around the City. The City Guide buses have a local guide on board to point out places of interest along the way. The City Hopper fare is just 20p wherever you want to go. You can just hop on any of the distinctive yellow buses, hand over yr 20p fare, and hop off again at any bus stop.

Many visitors really appreciate the journey by Hopper from the Waterfront to the Abbey – a walk of only half a mile but many, many steps!

A customised itinery will be drawn up and returned to you. Susan will even make ~~sure~~ all the arrangements for you if you wish. A fee of £10-£20 is charged according to the <u>complexity</u> ~~difficulty~~ ✓ of the task.

Move to Ⓐ

Two special supplements are published annually for sports lovers and music fans. These are sent to you automatically when you request a copy of the group guide. Dalefoot Stadium hosts many important sporting ∧ events – national and international.

The City Theatre and Royal Concert Hall are popular venues for performances covering the whole spectrum from opera to Oasis!

There's so much on offer in this famous Spa and the beautiful countryside of the surrounding area. Call us today to arrange yr ~~to~~ stay!

⊛

Don't forget to number the pages

Retrieve this document stored as EX11A. Save as UNIT11DOC2. Amend as indicated and print one copy.

PENNINE

KIRKDALE/SPA ← *Centre and underline*

The Guide is designed to help you ~~and your group~~ to get as much enjoyment as possible from your day out in Kirkdale/Spa. *Pennine*

You will find a complete list of local attractions including The Waterfront, Cedar Abbey and the City Art Gallery. Contact names, telephone numbers, admission prices and opening hours are given for each venue. ~~Many of our attractions offer special rates for groups. Please call the named official to receive help in ensuring an interesting and informative visit.~~ *emphasise this sentence* *Pennine*

The Tourist Information Office for Kirkdale/Spa and district will be happy to help you to plan an interesting and successful day ~~for your group;s visit~~. Simply telephone Susan Bywater on 01484-646 5636 with details of your ~~group numbers, ages,~~ special interests etc.

leave at least 1" (25mm) here

Consider the following alternatives:

City Art Gallery
Streamside Walk
The Waterfront
Maggie's Mill Shop
Cedar Abbey
Rowan Falls
Kirkdale Crafts

Sort into alphabetical order

Inset by 1" (25mm) at left

The Tourist Information Office is open as follows:-

Monday – Friday	9.30 am – 5.00 pm
Saturday and Sunday	10.00 am – 6.00 pm

Winter activities include tea dances in the Victoria Ballroom for the young at heart and the latest in winter sports technology at the Fellside Ski Slope for the young in body! There is a wide variety of accom in the area from first class hotels to modest self-catering establishments. Ask for details ~~before~~ you plan your outing – you may decide to stay over for 3 or 4 days!

Please key in the following table, save as UNIT11DOC3 and print one copy. Do not rule the table

KIRKDALE PENNINE SPA

ACCOM LIST ← (bold)

Accom grades are based on accessibility, cleanliness, ~~cleanlyness~~, type of accomodation and customer service standards. The price range is based on one person staying for one night except for self-catering prices which are shown as per week for the property. Hotel prices include bed, breakfast & evening meal.

Modify layout so that self-catering comes after B&B

TYPE OF ACCOM	ACCOM DETAILS		PRICE RANGE (£)
	GRADE	BEDROOMS	
Hotels			
Old Bank Hall	B	3	35.00 – 50.00
Linden House	C	5	30.00 – 49.00
Ellam Lodge	A	4	60.00 – 85.00
Sugden Howe	B	7	50.00 – 70.00
The Elms	A	10	60.00 – 90.00
Self-Catering			
Byrne Farm	C	2	90.00 – 200.00
Chapel End Cottage	C	2	110.00 – 210.00
The Grain Loft	A	1	200.00 – 350.00
Hill End	A	3	250.00 – 350.00
Peat Moor Barn	B	4	300.00 – 500.00
Bed and Breakfast			
Chapel End Farm	B	2	18.00 – 25.00
Whin Fell House	B	3	20.00 – 30.00
Beck Cottage	A	3	25.00 – 39.00
Low Stone Farm	B	2	20.00 – 35.00
Waterside Mill	B	4	19.00 – 29.00

Please sort into grade order (A first) in each section. Make sure all other details are also rearranged

Modify layout so that BEDROOMS becomes 2nd column

Please key in this memo, inserting phrases as shown. Save as UNIT11DOC4 and print as requested.

Use MEMOTEMP document and delete ACE Business Services

MEMORANDUM ← (centre and bold)

To: Susan Baywater, Tourist Info Office, Kirkdale P_S_

From: Kenneth Martin, Tourism Officer

Please check name and amend if necessary

Insert phrase stored as PHRASE11B

In yr part of the district, it is our intention to focus marketing research on group activities and facilities with a view to encouraging and expanding our provision. The new outdoor education ~~block~~ division at Dalefoot College will be working ~~alongside~~ with us on this ~~area~~ venture.

Insert phrase stored as PHRASE11C

Within the next few days, you should hear from Lyn Richard, Co-ordinator of Leisure and Recreation Programmes at D_ College. I hope that you and she can work together to oversee the students' research work.

I enclose a copy of the action plan.

Insert phrase stored as PHRASE11E

I think that you and your staff will enjoy working with the students. Obviously, they will need considerable guidance in the early stages and they will be supported by their College tutors. I have already spoken to the students allocated to your area. Many of them are local residents keen to help in developing facilities and opportunities on home ground. // I wish you and yr teams every success.

Top + 2 please. One copy for Lyn Richard; one for file. Indicate routing.

unit
12

► Introduction to
  Mailmerge

By the end of Unit 12, you should have learnt how to:

► set up a mailmerge operation
► create a mailmerge main document (form letter)
► create a mailmerge datafile (data source)
► add, delete and amend records in a mailmerge datafile
► merge a mailmerge main document with a datafile
► print merged documents.

 Mailmerge (or mail shot)

Mailmerge is the combining (merging) of data from two files into one file. The most common use of this feature is the production of 'personalised' letters. This feature would be useful when producing individual letters for all your customers or members. A generic letter would sound too impersonal, but to type out individual letters to everyone would be very time-consuming. Using mailmerge makes it much easier and quicker to carry out this task.

The two files used to operate a mailmerge are:

1) A **data file** – often a list of names, addresses and other details (This file is called the 'data source' in Word 97)

2) A **main document** – a letter or memo containing merge codes – merge codes are used to mark places where information from the data file will be inserted automatically (This file is called the 'form letter' in Word 97)

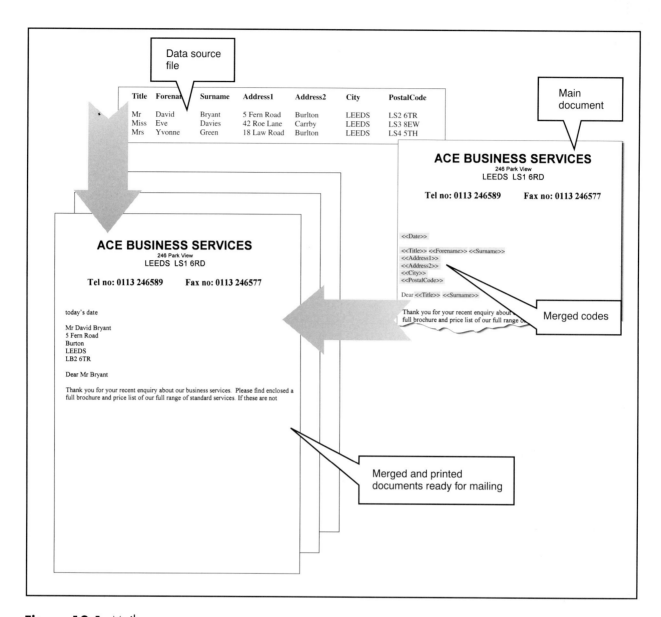

Figure 12.1 Mailmerge

In the RSA Mailmerge II Part 2 examination, you will normally be required to:

▶ retrieve, amend, sort and print one pre-stored datafile
▶ create, sort and print a second datafile
▶ create two main documents (one letter and one memo) to be merged with the above datafiles
▶ merge and print one set of individual mailmerge documents from each datafile, selecting on one criterion for one datafile and on more than one criterion for the second datafile.

Note: Although not required for the RSA examination, it is also possible to merge and print address labels and envelopes from a mailmerge datafile

Set up mailmerge

The following stages should be followed.

1 Create and name the main document (form letter).

2 Create the datafile (data source) – sorting and printing a copy if necessary.

3 Insert merge codes in the main document (form letter) – printing a copy if necessary.

4 Merge the data source and main document, if necessary selecting records from the data source on one or more criteria.

5 View and then print the merged documents.

Word 97's Mail Merge Helper dialogue box allows you to control the creation and manipulation of a mailmerge task.

 ## Create and name the main document (form letter)

The main document will contain text common to all recipients. The merge codes (indicating the position where personalised information is to be transferred from the data source) will be inserted at a later stage.

Mouse and menu

▶ Open: A **New** document
▶ Key in: The document text for your main document (letter or memo)
▶ Save: The main document using a suitable filename, eg **MAINDOC1** or **MAINDOC2** etc
▶ Select: **Tools**, **Mail Merge**

The Mail Merge Helper dialogue box is displayed on screen.

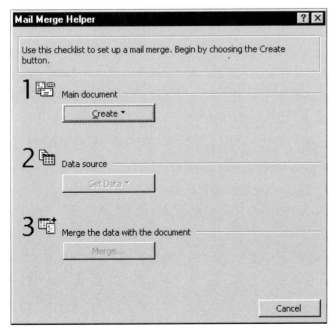

Figure 12.2 Mail Merge Helper dialogue box

▶ Click: **Create** in **Section 1 – Main Document**
▶ Select: **Form Letters** from the drop-down menu

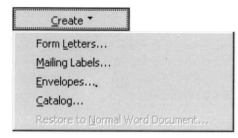

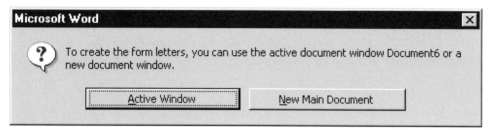

Figure 12.3 Create drop-down menu

The Form Letters dialogue box is displayed on screen.

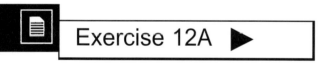

Figure 12.4 Form Letters dialogue box

▶ Click: **Active Window** – the Mail Merge Helper dialogue box is again displayed on screen (see Figure 12.1), ready for you to move to **Section 2 – Data Source**

The filename for the main document form letter is automatically displayed in Section 1 – Main Document.

Exercise 12A ▶

12.1 Following the instructions **Create and name the Main Document**, create a new main document by keying in the letter on the following page and saving it using the filename **UNIT12MAIN**. Use Times New Roman and font size 12.

Our Ref: GB/NS

Date of typing

Dear

Welcome to ACE Bodies, the in-house health and fitness club of ACE Business Services.

I have pleasure in enclosing your membership card and receipt for the membership fee. Hours of opening are shown on the card.

We look forward to seeing you soon for your introductory sessions where you will be given expert help in designing a practical and enjoyable exercise programme.

Yours sincerely

Gina Biondo
MANAGER

Encs

 ## Create the data source

The data source will contain a record for each addressee. Each record will be made up of 'fields', eg **Name**, **Address**, **Postcode**. Each field should contain the same kind of information.

After keying in the main document and naming this as the form letter for the mail merge operation, you are prompted to move to Section 2 – Data Source in the Mail Merge Helper dialogue box.

With the **Mail Merge Helper** dialogue box on screen:

▶ Click: **Get Data** in **Section 2 – Data Source**
▶ Select: **Create Data Source** from the drop-down menu

Figure 12.5 Get Data drop-down menu

The Create Data Source dialogue box is displayed on screen.

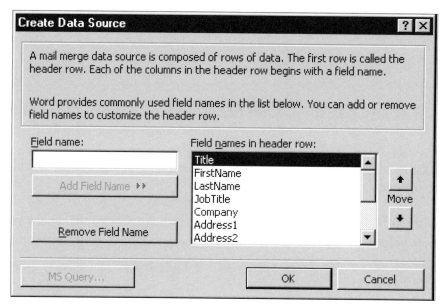

Figure 12.6 Create Data Source dialogue box

Word 97 has already provided some commonly-used field names – these are displayed in the **Field names in header row** menu box, eg **Title**, **FirstName**, **LastName**. Your data source will be much easier to use if it contains only the field names you require for the datafile you are creating. You can make the datafile fit your exact requirements by:

▶ removing any field names you do not require
▶ adding any field names you do require
▶ confirming the field names when you have completed the first two steps.

You may not require some field names, eg **State**

To remove unwanted field names from the Data Source:

▶ Select: The **Field Name** that is not required in the menu box
▶ Click: **Remove Field** Name

Repeat the above until all unwanted field names are removed.

You may require a field name which is not displayed in the given list, eg **Membership**

To add required field names to the Data Source:

▶ Key in: An appropriate name for the field in the **Field Name** box
   Note: a field name must begin with a letter and must not contain spaces.
▶ Click: **Add Field Name** to add your chosen field name to the list of **Field names in header row**

Repeat the above steps until all your additional fields have been named and each new field name has been added to the list.

Note: When you add a new field name to your data source, it is added at the bottom of the list of **Field names in header row**.

To move the field names into a different order:

The field names are transferred in the same order from this list to the data form and to the datafile when it is printed in table format. Your datafile may be much easier to use if the field names are in a logical order. You can move the field names as follows:

▶ Select: The field name to be moved
▶ Click: or ↑ on the **Move** section at the right of the **Field names in header row** menu box to move the field names to the required position in the list

When you have set up your datafile with the required field names and they are listed in the required order:

▶ Click: **OK** to confirm the field names displayed

Save the data source ▶

After confirming the field names selected for your data source, the Save As dialogue box is displayed on screen. If you are saving from View Source (Table) format then you will need to select **Save As** from the **File** menu.

▶ Select: An appropriate directory and drive in the **Save in** box
▶ Key in: An appropriate name in the **File name** box
▶ Click: **OK**

The Save Data Source dialogue box is displayed on screen.

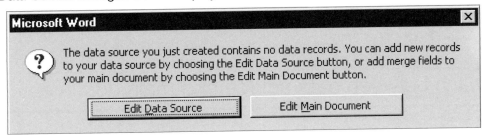

Figure 12.7 Save data source dialogue box

If you want to go straight to the **Data Form** and enter details for each record:

▶ Select: **Edit Data Source**

If you want to add merge fields to the form letter:

▶ Select: **Edit Main Document**

Exercise 12A continued ▶

12.2 With the main document **UNIT12MAIN** on screen and the **Mail Merge Helper** dialogue box displayed, refer to the instructions in **Create the data source** and create a data source file to be merged with the letter later, as follows:

a   **Remove the following Field names:**
JobTitle
Company
State
Country
HomePhone
WorkPhone

b   **Add the following Field name:**
Membership

c   **Practise changing the order of the field names in the Field names in Header row box.**
Arrange the Field names in the following order before proceeding:

Title
FirstName
LastName
Address1
Address2
City
PostalCode
Membership

12.3   Following the instructions **Save the Data Source**, save the data source you have just created as **UNIT12DATA1**.

After saving the document, select **Edit Data Source** from the dialogue box. Read the next two sections carefully, then go on to step 12.4.

 ## Switch between data source and main document ▶

When you have created a main document and a data source, the Mail Merge Helper dialogue box in Word 97 links the two files together. During the mail merge operation, you will need to switch between the two files. Refer to the following instructions while you are learning to carry out the Mail Merge operation in order to learn the different methods.

Using the Mail Merge Helper dialogue box

▶ Click: The **Mail Merge Helper** button on the Mail Merge Helper dialogue box

To switch to the Main Document:

▶ Click: The **Edit** button in **Section 1 – Main Document**

To switch to the Data Source (Data Form):

▶ Click: The **Mail Merge Helper** button on the Mail Merge Helper dialogue box
▶ Click: The **Edit** button in **Section 2 – Data Source**

Using the Database tool bar

Whilst in View Source (table format) mode, the Database Tool Bar is displayed on screen.

Figure 12.8 Database Tool Bar

To switch to the Main Document:

▶ Click: The **Mail Merge Main Document** button

To switch to the Data Source (Data Form):

▶ Click: The **Mail Merge Helper** button on the Mail Merge Helper dialogue box
▶ Click: The **Data Form** button

Using the Window option on the Main menu

To switch to the Main Document:

▶ Click: **Window** on the **Main** menu
▶ Select: The **Main Document** filename

To switch to the Datafile:

▶ Click: **Window** on the **Main** menu
▶ Select: The **Datafile** filename

Edit the data source (enter the record files) ▶

▶ Unless the Data Form is already on your screen, use one of the methods described in **Switching between the Main Document and the Data Source** to access the appropriate Data Source.

The Data Form is displayed on screen.

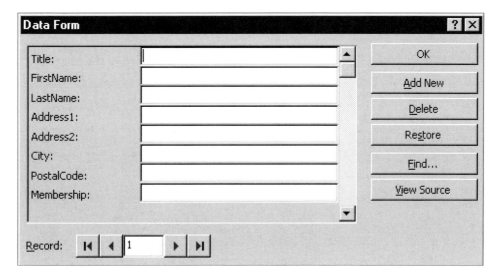

Figure 12.9 Data Form

1 Key in: The information for the first field

2 Press: ↵ (return/enter) to enter the information and move to the next field

3 Repeat: Steps 1–2 until all fields for the first record are entered

4 Click: **Add New**

5 Repeat: Steps 1–3 for each record

When all records are entered:

▶ Click: **OK**

Options available in the data form

Button	Action
Record	Move to another record by keying in the appropriate record number, *or* Click: **First Record**, **Previous Record**, **Next Record**, or **Last Record**
Delete	Deletes the current record
Restore	Reverses changes made to the current record
Find	Searches for specified data throughout records
View Source	Displays all records in the form of a table

 Exercise 12A continued ▶

12.4 Following the instructions **Edit the Data Source**, enter the four records shown under **Exercise 12A – records for data source** into the Data Form (4 records).

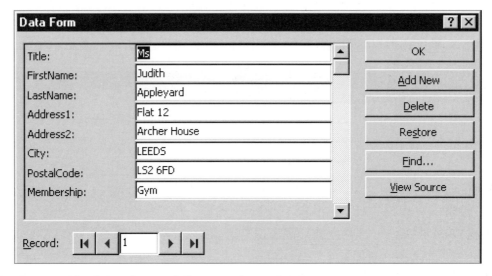

Figure 12.10 Example of data form with first record completed

Exercise 12A – records for data source

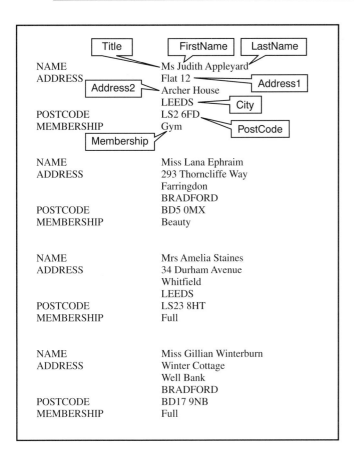

NAME	Ms Judith Appleyard
ADDRESS	Flat 12
	Archer House
	LEEDS
POSTCODE	LS2 6FD
MEMBERSHIP	Gym

Field labels pointing to the record above: Title, FirstName, LastName, Address2, Address1, City, PostCode, Membership

NAME	Miss Lana Ephraim
ADDRESS	293 Thorncliffe Way
	Farringdon
	BRADFORD
POSTCODE	BD5 0MX
MEMBERSHIP	Beauty

NAME	Mrs Amelia Staines
ADDRESS	34 Durham Avenue
	Whitfield
	LEEDS
POSTCODE	LS23 8HT
MEMBERSHIP	Full

NAME	Miss Gillian Winterburn
ADDRESS	Winter Cottage
	Well Bank
	BRADFORD
POSTCODE	BD17 9NB
MEMBERSHIP	Full

Try to remember not to press the spacebar after entering data into a field. Press return immediately after the last letter to avoid extra spaces when your letter is merged with the datafile.

Save and print the data source

You may be required to produce a printout of the records in your data source – at work as well as in examinations.

Using one of the methods described in Switching between the Main Document and the Data Source, access the appropriate Data Source.

▶ Click: The **View Source** button in the Data Form dialogue box

The Data Source file is displayed on screen. You may find that some of the text wraps illogically in the boxes to allow all the information to be displayed. This format is acceptable in RSA examinations – you do not have to reformat the table layout.

▶ Select: **Print** from the **File** menu and print in the normal way
▶ Select: **Save** from the **File** menu to save the completed datafile

Note: The data source printout checks in this book have been reproduced in the same font size as the documents, ie Times New Roman, font size 12. Your software may be set up with a different font size as default, ie font size 10. There is no need for you to change the font size when you print your data source as any size is acceptable in examinations as long as it is not too small to be legible.

12.5 Resave your document and print one copy of the datafile. Check your work very carefully, comparing it with the printout check at the back of the book. If you find any errors, retrieve the data source and correct them now before proceeding further with your mailmerge.

 # Insert merge codes in the main document

The main document and data source are linked through the Mail Merge Helper dialogue box when mail merge is set up. Word 97 will transfer data from the data source to the main document, selecting the data by record and then by field. Merge codes in the main document indicate the position and type of data which is to be transferred from the data source.

Using one of the methods described under **Switching between data source and main document** make sure that your Main Document Form Letter is displayed on screen and that the Mail Merge Tool Bar is also on screen.

Figure 12.11 Mail Merge Tool Bar

▶ Move the cursor: To the position where you wish to enter the first merge code in the main document
▶ Click: The **Insert Merge** Field button on the Mail Merge Tool Bar
▶ Select: The required field name from the drop-down menu (Figure 12.12.)
▶ Repeat: Steps 1–3 for each subsequent merge field code required

Figure 12.12 Field names drop-down menu

Note: Merge codes can be formatted after being inserted into the main document.

▶ Click: On the merge code text in your main document to check that the font size of the merge codes is the same as the remainder of the document
▶ Use: Bold, underline, italic etc if the data requires emphasis

12.6 Following the instructions **Insert merge codes in the main document**, insert merge codes in your main document as shown below. Check that the merge code text and letter text is in the same font and size.

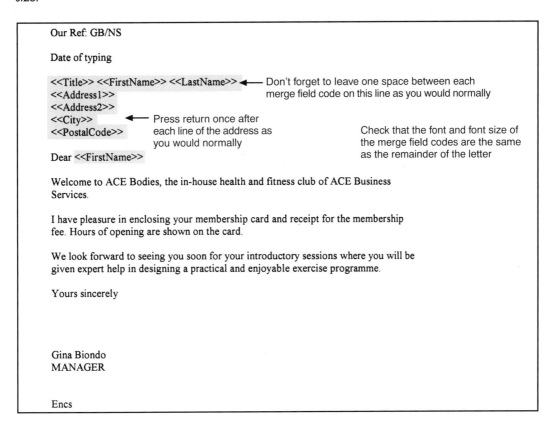

Our Ref: GB/NS

Date of typing

<<Title>> <<FirstName>> <<LastName>> ◄— Don't forget to leave one space between each
<<Address1>>   merge field code on this line as you would normally
<<Address2>>
<<City>>   ◄— Press return once after
<<PostalCode>>   each line of the address as   Check that the font and font size of
                     you would normally   the merge field codes are the same
                                                          as the remainder of the letter
Dear <<FirstName>>

Welcome to ACE Bodies, the in-house health and fitness club of ACE Business Services.

I have pleasure in enclosing your membership card and receipt for the membership fee. Hours of opening are shown on the card.

We look forward to seeing you soon for your introductory sessions where you will be given expert help in designing a practical and enjoyable exercise programme.

Yours sincerely

Gina Biondo
MANAGER

Encs

Print the form letter ▶

You may be required to produce a printout of the form letter – at work as well as in examinations.

With the form letter displayed on screen:

▶ Print in the normal way
▶ Select: **Save** from the **File** menu to save the completed main document

12.7 Resave the main document including the merge codes. Print a copy of the form letter. Check your work with the printout check at the back of the book. Correct any errors which you find before proceeding.

View the merged file ▶

In the Main Document window:

Click: The **View Merged Data** button on the Mail Merge Tool Bar

The first merged document is displayed on screen.

To view other records:

▶ Click: The | ◄ ◄ | 2 | ► | ►| arrow buttons on the Mail Merge Tool Bar, *or*
▶ Key in: The number of the required record in the box between the arrows

To return to the main document:

▶ Click: The **View Merged Data** button on the Mail Merge Tool Bar again

 ## Print the merged file ▶

To print all merged documents:

▶ Click: The **Merge to Printer** button on the Mail Merge Tool Bar

To print one merged letter, eg for checking purposes:

▶ Select: **Current page** in the **Page range** section of the Print dialogue box

 ## Exercise 12A continued ▶

12.8 Following the instructions **View the merged file**, merge the main document and the data source. Check the merged documents carefully – four personalised letters should have been processed. If you need to make amendments, switch back to the main document to do this so that your amendments will apply to all of the mailmerged documents.

12.9 Print only the letter to Lana Ephraim by placing the cursor in this document and selecting **Current Page** in the Print dialogue box. Check your printout of the letter to Lana Ephraim against the printout check at the back of the book. If you find any errors, switch back to the main document or the datafile to correct them so that your amendments will apply to all of the mailmerged documents.

 ## Amend records ▶

It may be necessary for you to make amendments to the records in your data source as circumstances change, eg a change of address.

Method 1 – using the find record function in the data source

Word 97 allows you to find a particular record without scanning through every record. This is useful for making amendments to individual records.

Using one of the methods described in **Switching between the main document and the data source**, access the appropriate Data Source.

With the Data Form displayed on screen:

▶ Click: **Find**

OR with the Data Source in View Source format, ie table format:

▶ Click: The 🔍 **Find Record** button on the Database Tool Bar

The Find in Field dialogue box is displayed on screen.

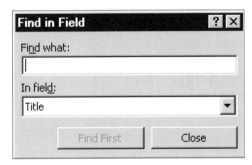

Figure 12.13 Find in Field dialogue box

▶ Key in: The data which you wish to amend, eg Brown if you want to change this name to Browne
▶ Select: The field in which this is situated in the **In field** box, eg Name
▶ Click on: **Find First**

Note: Word 97 will display the first record containing the specified data in the specified field. You should check other details such as address or date of birth within the record to help you to find the exact record you require as there may be several records with the name 'Brown'.

▶ Click: **Find Next** until you locate the correct record
▶ Click: **Close**
▶ Key in: The new (amended) data
▶ Click: **Find** to select the next record to be amended
▶ Click: **OK** when all amendments to all records are completed

Method 2 – using the view source (table)

Word 97 allows you to make amendments to records while they are displayed on screen in table format. This is useful if an additional field has been added and you wish to enter data into this field in each record. If the data is often the same, eg weekly or monthly, you could use the copy and paste facility to insert the data.

With the Data Form displayed on screen:

▶ Click: The **View Source** button in the **Data Form** dialogue box

The data source is displayed on screen in the form of a table.

▶ Amend the data as required, adding, deleting and changing as necessary

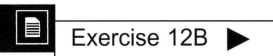
12.10 Using **Method 1 – Find Record in Data Source**, find the following records by keying in the LastName. Save as **UNIT12DATA2**. Then amend the records as shown below:

NAME   Mrs Amelia Staines
ADDRESS   ~~34 Durham Avenue~~
               Whitfield   124 York Rd
               LEEDS
POSTCODE   LS23 8HT
MEMBERSHIP   Full

                        Gill
NAME   Miss ~~Gillian~~ Winterburn
ADDRESS   Winter Cottage
               Well Bank
               BRADFORD
POSTCODE   BD17 9NB
MEMBERSHIP   Full

Add and delete records ▶

It may be necessary for you to add new records and also to delete records from your data source as circumstances change, eg employee or member joining or leaving an organisation.

Using one of the methods described in **Switching between the main document and the data source**, access the appropriate Data Source.

To delete a record from the data source:

Find the appropriate record by using one of the Find options described in **Amending the records**

▶ Click: The **Delete** button in the **Data Form** dialogue box

OR with the View Source (Table) format on screen:

▶ Select: The Record to be deleted
▶ Click: The **Delete Record** button on the Database Tool Bar

To add a new record to the data source:

With the Data Form on screen:

▶ Click: **Add New** to move to a blank record
▶ Key in: The record details
▶ Click: **Add New**

With the View Source (Table) format on screen:

▶ Click: The **Add New Record** button on the Database Tool Bar
▶ Key in: The record details in the blank row created

Exercise 12B continued ▶

12.11 Referring to the instructions **To delete a record from the data source**, delete the record for Judith Appleyard.

12.12 Referring to the instructions **To add a new record to the data source**, add the following new members:

NAME	Ms Saira Mistry
ADDRESS	3 The Crescent
	Eastfield
	LEEDS
POSTCODE	LS10 3JW
MEMBERSHIP	Gym
NAME	Mrs Fiona McLeod
ADDRESS	The Coach House
	Hallenshaw
	BRADFORD
POSTCODE	BD16 7HH
MEMBERSHIP	Beauty
NAME	Miss Marie Bonney
ADDRESS	7 Severn Street
	Whitfield
	LEEDS
POSTCODE	LS23 6DD
MEMBERSHIP	Gym

12.13 Resave the data source and print one copy of the datafile. Check this carefully with the printout check at the back of the book. If you find any errors, retrieve the data source and correct them.

Exercise 12C

12.14 Following the instructions in **View the merged file** and **Print the merged file**, merge and print letters to all 6 new members of the **Ace Bodies Club**. Check your documents against the printout checks at the back of the book. If you find any errors, retrieve the data source or the main documents and make any necessary corrections in these files so that amendments will be effective in all merged documents.

12.15 Exit the program if you have finished working or continue on to the next unit.

unit 13

▶ Manipulating data in Mailmerge

By the end of Unit 13 you should have learnt how to:

▶ add and delete fields in a mailmerge data source

▶ sort a mailmerge data source into alphabetical and numerical order

▶ select records by one or more criteria from a mailmerge data source

▶ merge a main document with selected records

▶ print a main document merged with selected records.

 ## Amend the data source fields ▶

It may be necessary for you to make amendments to the data source fields so that you can store additional data or delete data that is no longer required.

Open the data source file you wish to amend in the usual way. The View Source (table format) is usually displayed. If it is not displayed:

▶ Click: The **View Source** button in the **Data Form** dialogue box

▶ Check: That the Database Tool Bar (Figure 13.1) is displayed on screen.

If it is not displayed:

▶ Select: **Tool Bars** from the **View** menu

▶ Select: **Database** (a ✔ will appear next to the word when it is selected)

The Database Tool Bar is displayed on the screen.

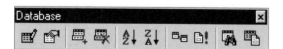

Figure 13.1 Database Tool Bar

▶ Click: The **Manage Fields** button on the Database Tool Bar

The Manage Fields dialogue box is displayed on screen.

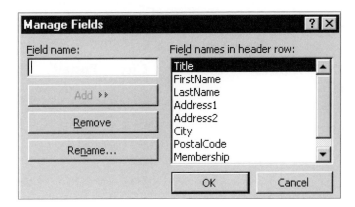

Figure 13.2 Manage Fields dialogue box

▶ Select: The field name you wish to amend in the **Field name in header row** box, *or*
▶ Key in: The field name you wish to amend in the **Field name** box

Options available in Manage Fields dialogue box

Button	Action
Add	Add a new field name to the data source
Remove	Remove a field name from the data source
Rename	Rename an existing field in the data source

▶ Click: **OK** to confirm amendments

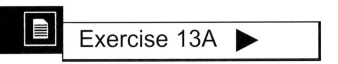

Exercise 13A ▶

13.1 Retrieve the data source file stored under the filename **UNIT12DATA2**. Save as **UNIT13DATA1**.

13.2 Following the instructions **Amending the data source fields**, refer to the following data source printout and add an extra field name **Sub due date**.

13.3 Refer back to the instructions given in Unit 12 in **Amending the records**, and complete Exercise 13A by altering all the records as shown on the next page, adding relevant data for the new field and making other amendments as shown. You may choose to amend the records in Data Form format or in View Source (Table) format.

Add this field to the database

Title	First Name	LastName	Address 1	Address 2	City	PostalCode	Membership	Sub due date
Miss	Lana	Ephraim	293 Thorncliffe Way	Farringdon	BRADFORD RD	BD5 0MX	Beauty	31/12/98
Mrs	Amelia	Staines	124 York Road	Whitfield	LEEDS	LS23 8HT	Beauty ~~Full~~	31/12/98
~~Miss~~ Mrs	Gill ✔	~~Winterburn~~ Brooke	~~Winter Cottage~~ Grafton House	Well Bank ✔	BRADFORD RD ✔	BD17 ~~9NB~~ 9BH	Full ✔	31/7/98
Ms	Saira	Mistry	3 The Crescent	Eastfield	LEEDS	LS10 3JW	Gym	30/6/98
Mrs	Fiona	McLeod	The Coach House	Hallenshaw	BRADFORD RD	BD16 7HH	~~Beauty~~ Full	31/12/98
Miss	Marie	Bonney	7 Severn Street	Whitfield	LEEDS	LS23 6DD	Gym	30/4/98

Use the format shown here for the dates

13.4 Save the data source and print one copy of the datafile. Check your work very carefully, comparing it with the printout check at the back of the book. If you find any errors, retrieve the data source and correct them now before proceeding further with your mailmerge.

Sort the data source

It may be necessary for you to sort the data source to present the information in a useful way.

Open the data source file you wish to amend in the usual way. The View Source (table format) is usually displayed. If it is not displayed:

▶ Click: The **View Source** button in the **Data Form** dialogue box
▶ Check: That the Database Tool Bar (Figure 13.3) is displayed on screen.

If it is not displayed:

▶ Select: **Tool Bars** from the **View** menu
▶ Select: **Database** (a ✔ will appear next to the word when it is selected)

The Database Tool Bar is displayed on the screen.

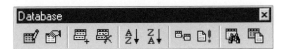

Figure 13.3 Database Tool Bar

▶ Place the cursor: In the column representing the field by which the data source is to be sorted
▶ Click: The 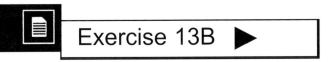 **Sort ascending** or the **Sort descending** button on the Database Tool Bar as appropriate

---

Exercise 13B ▶

13.5 Retrieve the data source stored as **UNIT13DATA1** unless it is already on screen. Following the instructions in **Sort the data source**, sort the data into ascending (A–Z) alphabetical order of LastName and print one copy. Check your work with the printout check at the back of the book, and repeat the procedure if necessary.

13.6 Sort the data into descending (Z–A) order by **Sub due date** and print one copy. Check your work with the printout check at the back of the book and repeat the procedure if necessary.

13.7 Resave the data source and close the file.

Open the mailmerge data source ▶

The main document and data source are linked when mail merge is set up. Word 97 will transfer data from the data source to the main document, selecting the data by record and then by field. The Mail Merge Helper dialogue box helps you to link the two files together.

With the main document on screen:

▶ Select: **Tools, Mail Merge**
▶ Click: **Get Data** in the **2 – Data Source** section of the Mail Merge Helper dialogue box
▶ Click: **Open Data Source**
▶ Select: The required **Data Source** from the listed files

The following dialogue box is displayed on screen.

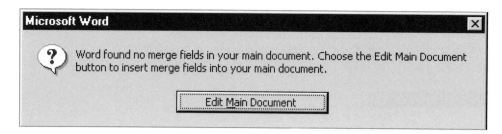

Figure 13.4 No Merge Fields dialogue box

▶ Select: **Edit Main Document**

Exercise 13C ▶

13.8 Re-read the instructions given in Unit 12 in **Create and name the main document** and in **Open the mail merge data source** in this Unit. You are going to start a new mail merge operation by using the active window as your main document. This will be merged with the data source stored as **UNIT13DATA1**. Follow the steps 13.9–13.12.

13.9 Open a new document. Select **File** from the **Insert** menu, and insert the letterhead file saved as **LETTERTEMP** into your document.

13.10 Key in the letter on the next page using Times New Roman, font size 12. Referring back to the instructions in Unit 12 in **Insert merge codes in the main document**, insert merge codes in the letter where indicated by *, eg *****Title**.

Our Ref: GB/DB

Date of typing

*Title *FirstName *LastName
*Address1
*Address2
*City
*PostalCode

Dear *FirstName

'ACE BODIES' – MEMBERSHIP DETAILS

As I am sure you already know, our in-house health and fitness club has been a tremendous success. Since starting up 6 months ago with approximately 25 brave and energetic employees, our membership has grown to over 150! The most popular activities are still multi-gym and exercise classes of various types but the beauty therapy section is expanding quickly and extra evening sessions are to begin next month.

We have recently computerised our membership records (with considerable help from Louise Allersby in Computer Operations). This letter has been produced to allow us to check your details. Your membership type and subscription due date are shown below:

Membership: *Membership   Subscription due date: *Sub due date

Please inform us if this information is not correct so that we can amend it. We would also like to hear from you if your name and address details are incorrect in any way. If we do not hear from you, we will assume we got it right!

Thank you for your co-operation and wishing you the best of health.

Yours sincerely

Gina Biondo
MANAGER

13.11 Save the form letter you have just created as **UNIT13CMAIN**, and print one copy. Check your work with the printout check at the back of the book and correct any errors before proceeding.

13.12 Referring back to the instructions in Unit 12 in **View the merged file**, merge the main document and the data source. Check the merged documents carefully – six personalised letters should have been processed. If you need to make any amendments, switch back to the main document to do this so that your amendments will apply to all of the merged documents.

When the merged documents are correct, return to the main document by:

▶ Clicking on the **View Merged Data** button on the Mail Merge Tool Bar, *or*

▶ Selecting **Close** from the **File** menu (not saving changes).

 ## Select specific records to be merged using one criterion ▶

You may be requested to merge a form letter with a selection of the data source records which match one specific criterion.

▶ Click: The **Mail Merge Helper** button on the Mail Merge Tool Bar

▶ Click: The ⎸ Query Options... ⎹ **Query Options** button in **Section 3 – Merge the data with the document**

The Query Options dialogue box is displayed on screen.

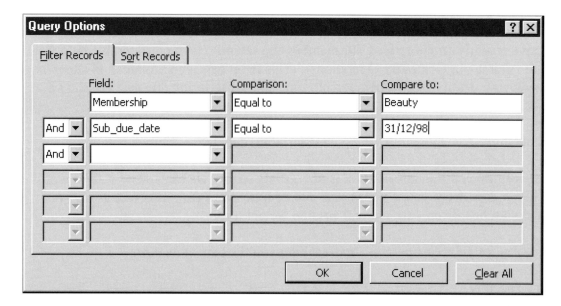

Figure 13.5   Query Options dialogue box

▶ Select: The field to which you want to apply a criterion from the drop-down menu in the **Field** box

▶ Select: **Equal to** from the drop-down menu in the **Comparison** box (Other options such as **Less than**, **Greater than** and **Not equal to** are also available)

▶ Key in: The required criterion in the **Compare To** box

▶ Click: **OK**

▶ Click: **Merge** in **Section 3 – Merge the data with the document**

The Merge dialogue box is displayed on screen.

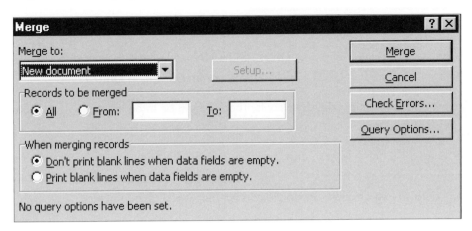

Figure 13.6 Merge dialogue box

▶ Select: **New Document** in the **Merge To** box
▶ Check: That **Don't print blank lines when data fields are empty** is selected (ie has a black circle in it)
▶ Click: The **Merge** button
▶ View: The merged file to check selection before printing
▶ Print, save and close the merged file

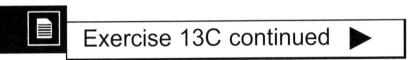

Exercise 13C continued ▶

13.13 Following the instructions in **Select specific records to be merged using one criterion**, merge the main document with the records for **Full** members only:

▶ Click: The **Mail Merge Helper** button on the Mail Merge Tool Bar
▶ Click: **Query Options** in Section 3 of the Mail Merge Helper dialogue box
▶ Select: Membership from the Field drop-down menu
▶ Select: **Equal to** in the **Comparison** box
▶ Key in: **Full** in the **Compare to** box
▶ Click: **OK**
▶ Click: **Merge**
▶ Select: **New Document** in the **Merge** to box of the Merge dialogue box
▶ Click: **Merge**

13.14 View the merged file to check the documents. There should be two letters – one to Fiona McLeod and one to Gill Brooke.

13.15 Print the merged file (two letters). Check your letters with the printout check at the back of the book. If you find any errors, switch back to the mail merge helper dialogue box and then to the main document, data source or query options to correct your work. Close the file.

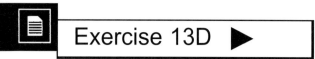

Exercise 13D ▶

13.16 Retrieve the main document stored as **UNIT13CMAIN** and merge the main document with the records in the data source stored as **UNIT13DATA2** for members living in **LEEDS** only.

13.17 View the merged file to check the documents. There should be three letters: to Amelia Staines, Saira Mistry and Marie Bonney.

13.18 Print the merged file (three letters), and check your work with the printout check at the back of the book. If you find any errors, switch back to the mail merge helper dialogue box and then to the main document, data source or query options to correct your work. Close the file.

Select specific records to be merged using two criteria

You may be requested to merge a form letter with a selection of the data source records which match two (or more) specific criteria.

▶ Click: The **Mail Merge Helper** button on the Mail Merge Tool Bar

▶ Click: The **Query Options** button in Section 3

The Query Options dialogue box is displayed on screen

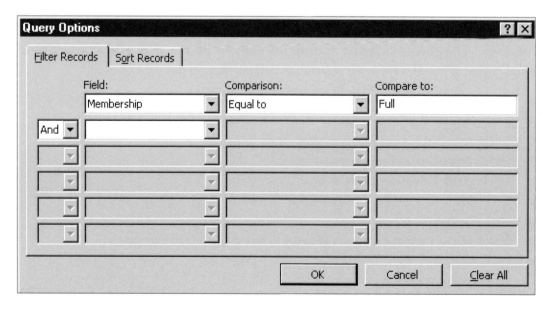

Figure 13.7 Query Options dialogue box

▶ Select: The appropriate field from the drop-down menu in the **Field** box
▶ Select: **Equal** to from the drop-down menu in the **Comparison** box (Other options such as **Less than**, **Greater than** and **Not equal to** are also available)
▶ Key in: The required criterion in the **Compare To** box
▶ Repeat: The above procedure for the second criterion
▶ Click: **OK**

▶ Close: Mail Merge Helper dialogue box

▶ View: The merged file to check the selection before printing (The number of selected records is displayed on the Mail Merge Tool Bar)

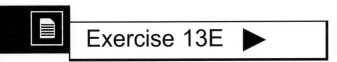

Exercise 13E ▶

13.19 Retrieve the main document stored as **UNIT13CMAIN** and merge the main document with the records in the data source stored as **UNIT13DATA2** for **Beauty** membership whose subscription due date is **31/12/98**. The Query Options dialogue box should appear as in figure 13.7.

13.20 View the merged file to check the documents. There should be two letters – to Amelia Staines and Lana Ephraim.

13.21 Print the merged file (two letters). Close the file.

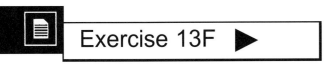

Exercise 13F ▶

13.22 Using the same main document and datafile, merge the main document with the records for **Gym** members living in **Leeds**.

13.23 View the merged file to check the documents. There should be two letters – to Saira Mistry and Marie Bonney.

13.24 Print the merged file (two letters). Close the file.

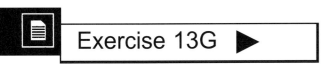

Exercise 13G ▶

13.25 Save the data source as **UNIT13DATA3**. Following the instructions in **Amend the data source fields** remove the **Title** and **Membership** fields from the data source:

▶ Switch to the data source if not already on screen

▶ Switch to View Source (Table) format

▶ Click: **Manage fields** on the Database Tool Bar

▶ Remove: The **Title** field

▶ Remove: The **Membership** field

13.26 Print a copy of the data source. Check your work with the printout check at the back of the book. Resave the amended data source.

13.27 Exit the program if you have finished working or continue on to the next unit.

By the end of Unit 14, you should have revised and practised all the techniques and skills needed for the RSA Mailmerge Stage II Part 2 Award.

Look at your Progress Review Checklist and at your completed exercises to remind yourself of what you have learnt so far and to identify any weaknesses. Then complete the following exercises as revision.

 Exercise 14A

> Please key in the following records as a datafile suitable for use with the memo in Exercise 14B. Save as EX14ADATA and print one copy.

Roche	Akhtar
Sandra	Saima
37 Denfield Ave	26 Shaw Rd
Farringdon	Whitfield
BRADFORD	LEEDS
BD5 5NQ	LS23 8EL
Sales	Purchasing
Roper	Broadbent
James	Roger
Hill Crest	Hebble View
Hallenshaw	Hallenshaw
BRADFORD	BRADFORD
BD16 3RF	BD16 8JT
Accounts	Sales

Loboda
Francis
17 Moorend Grove
Whitfield
LEEDS
LS23 5SL
Production

Charnock
Alicia
10 Westgate
Well Bank
BRADFORD
BD17 3LW
Sales

Hartley
Shirley
160 Sandhall Rd
Well Bank
BRADFORD
BD17 2RA
Sales

Dale
Colin
1 Cromwell Drive
Farringdon
BRADFORD
BD5 4NS
Accounts

Blagbrough
Alan
13 New Street
Eastfield
LEEDS
LS10 9SD
Marketing

Fitzgerald
Sonia
16 Arncliffe Lane
Dalefoot
BRADFORD
BD21 2LD
Marketing

Exercise 14B

Key in the standard document (memo) on the next page to be merged with the datafile created in Exercise 14A.

▶ Use the **Memotemp** memorandum head
▶ Use a ragged right margin
▶ Insert merge codes where indicated by *
▶ Save as **EX14BMAIN** and print one copy of the standard document
▶ Merge the standard document with the data source stored as **EX14ADATA** and filter the records to print memos to Sales Department staff only

MEMO

(Please retain commas)

To: *FirstName *LastName, *Dept Department
From: Simon Queensbury, Personnel Administrator

Staff Induction ← (emphasise heading)

Welcome to ACE! I hope that your first few days with us have been interesting and enjoyable, and that you are beginning to settle in to the department and the Company.

In addition to the ~~usual~~ Health and Safety and Departmental ~~Awareness raising~~ Induction sessions, we are planning an induction morning to give more details of our expansion plans and to allow you to see more of other departments and personnel.

Please come along to the Board Room at 10.00 am on Tuesday 10 May. Coffee and biscuits will be served and the meeting should be finished at approximately 12 noon.

I enclose some literature for you to read prior to the meeting and look forward to seeing you on the date given above.

Enc

Recall this datafile stored under EX14DATA and save as EX14CDATA. Amend as indicated and sort the amended datafile into alphabetical order of surname. Print one copy. This datafile will be required for use with Exercise 14D.

Please add these fields to each record → Grade, Appraisal, Payroll

Please delete this record → (Blagbrough row)

See separate sheet for additional records to be included in this file

LastName	FirstName	Address1	Address2	City	PostalCode	Dept	Grade	Appraisal	Payroll
Roche	Sandra	37 Denfield ~~Avenue~~ Grove	Farringdon	BRADFORD	BD5 5NQ	Sales	B	Aug	01021
Roper	~~James~~ Jim	Hill Crest	Hallenshaw	BRADFORD	BD16 3RF	Accounts	D	July	01022
Loboda	Francis	17 Moorend Grove	Whitfield	LEEDS	LS23 5SL	Production	D	Aug	01023
Hartley	Shirley	~~160~~ 16 Sandhall Road	Well Bank	BRADFORD	BD17 2RA	Sales	D	July	01024
~~Blagbrough~~	~~Alan~~	~~13 New Street~~	~~Eastfield~~	~~LEEDS~~	~~LS10 9SD~~	~~Marketing~~			~~01025~~
Akhtar	Saima	26 Shaw Road	Whitfield	LEEDS	LS23 8EL	Purchasing	D	July	01026
Broadbent	Roger	Hebble View	Hallenshaw	BRADFORD	BD16 8JT	Sales	A	July	01027
Charnock	Alicia	10 Westgate	Well Bank	BRADFORD	BD17 3LW	Sales	D	Aug	01028
Dale	Colin	1 Cromwell Drive	Farringdon	BRADFORD	BD5 4NS	Accounts	E	July	01029
Fitzgerald	~~Sonia~~ Sonya	16 Arncliffe Lane	Dalefoot	BRADFORD	BD21 2LD	Marketing	B	Aug	~~010~~ 01210

Please add the records shown below to the datafile before sorting and printing

Dept	Name	Address	Grade	Appraisal	Payroll
Accounts	Calvert, Margaret	10 Ramsden Row, Dalefoot, BFD, BD21 4SE	C	May	00182
Purchasing	Fielden, Jonathan	5 South Parade, Whitfield, LDS, LS23 7NP	D	July	00437
Marketing	Lawrence, Sarah	Highcroft, Burn Wood, BFD, BD19 3AL	D	April	00449
	Petrovic, Tadeusz	Green House, Hallenshaw, BFD, BD16 2EN	C	April	00132
(Personnel)	Sawyer, Kevin	17 Badger Ln, Hollins, LDS, LS3 6HB	B	Jan	00642
	James, Iain	131 Lodge Gro, Stonemount, BFD, BD10 9RA	E	June	00997
	Clare, Alison	Dale Head, Burn Wood, BFD, BD19 7DH	A	Aug	00201
	Lewis, Katy	Howard Hall, Dalefoot, BFD, BD21 5RT	B	Sept	00236
	Shuvla, Milo	14 Cook St, Eastfield, LDS, LS10 4EA	D	July	00239
	Sykes, William	2 Oliver's Way, Arden, LDS, LS6 8RD	B	Dec	00690
	Southgate, Daniel	11 George St, Whitfield, LDS, LS23 1TV	D	July	00592
Production	Zimmer, Marc	4 Woodhouse Rd, Burnwood, BFD, BD19 9SH	E	Dec	00671
	Woodhead, Steven	4 Woodview Ave, Well Bank, BFD, BD17 7LA	C	Jan	00668
	Morris, Graham	60 Sharby Dr, Dalefoot, BFD, BD21 5LV	A	Mar	00144
	Woodhead, Lee	52 Wakefield Rd, Farringdon, BFD, BD5 2DB	D	July	00789
	Khan, Sofina	13 Whalley Rd, Eastfield, LDS, LS10 4WA	D	July	00682
Sales	Sykes, Valerie	2 Oliver's Way, Arden, LDS, LS6 8RD	D	July	00591
	Gannon, Kathleen	8 Lea Gro, Well Bank, BFD, BD17 7JS	E	Mar	00876
	Reed, Adam	8 Grange Rd, Stonemount, BFD, BD10 1NS	C	Feb	00672
	Khalid, Nukhtar	13 South Parade, Whitfield, LDS, LS23 7PR	B	Oct	00434

Please put cities BRADFORD and LEEDS in full throughout

Key in the following standard document (letter) to be merged with the datafile amended in Exercise 14C.

▶ Use the **Lettertemp** letterhead
▶ Insert merge codes at *
▶ Use a justified right margin
▶ Save as **EX14DMAIN** and print one copy of the standard document
▶ Merge with the data source saved as **EX14CDATA** and print letters only to **Grade D** employees whose appraisal month is **July**.

* FirstName *LastName
* Address1
* Address2
* City
* PostalCode

Dear *FirstName

Annual Appraisal ← (please emphasise)

I am writing to remind you that your annual appraisal ~~interview~~ discussion is to take place in * Appraisal. Grade *grade members of staff are to be appraised for the first time this year following consultation and information sessions.

Unless otherwise agreed, your immediate line manager will be your appraiser and preliminary meetings will take place approximately 4 weeks beforehand.

A full pack of documentation was issued during the earlier information session. If you require further copies, please contact me on Extension 242.

Yrs sncly

Simon Queensbury
Personnel Administrator

unit
15

▶ Examination Practice 3

By the end of Unit 15, you should have completed a mock examination for the RSA Stage II Part 2 Mailmerge Award.

RSA Stage II Part 2 Mailmerge ▶

This examination assesses your ability to create, maintain and print datafiles and standard documents, and to print selected merged documents using merge facilities. The award demonstrates that you have acquired competence in operating mailmerge.

The examination lasts for $1\frac{1}{2}$ hours and you have to prepare and manipulate two datafiles and create two documents for use in two mailmerge operations. Printing is done outside this time.

Examinations are carried out in registered centres and are marked by RSA examiners. The centre will give you instructions regarding stationery. Letters must be produced on letterheads (either pre-printed or a template) and memos may be produced on pre-printed forms, by keying in entry details or by use of a template. The invigilator will give you instructions concerning the recalling of stored files.

Examination hints

When sitting your examination:

▶ you may use a manual prepared by the centre or the software manufacturer
▶ put your name, centre number and document number on each document
▶ check your work very carefully before printing – proofread, spellcheck
▶ assemble your printouts in the correct order at the end of the examination.

You are now ready to try a mock examination for Mailmerge Stage II Part 2. Take care and good luck!

The list of assessment criteria for this examination is long and detailed. To be sure that you have reached the required standard to be entered for an examination, you need to work through several past papers and have these 'marked' by a tutor or assessor who is qualified and experienced in this field.

Results

▶ If your finished work has 3 faults or fewer, you will be awarded a distinction.
▶ If your finished work has between 4 and 7 faults, you will be awarded a pass.
▶ Results are sent to the centre where you sit your examination.

Recall this datafile stored as EX14CDATA, and save as UNIT15 DATA. Add new records and a new field and amend records as shown. Sort into alphabetical order of grade and then alphabetically by surname within each grade. Save as UNIT 15 DATA. Print one copy. This datafile will be required for use with Document 3.

(Please add this field to each record)

LastName	FirstName	Address1	Address2	City	PostalCode	Dept	Grade	Appraisal	Payroll	Car Reg
Akhtar	Saima	26 Shaw Road	Whitfield	LEEDS	LS23 8EL	~~Sales~~ Sales	~~D~~ C	July	01026	L446 BOL
Broadbent	Roger	Hebble View	Hallenshaw	BRADFORD	BD16 8JT	~~Purchasing~~ Sales	A	July	01027	P67 DAP
Calvert	Margaret	10 Ramsden Row	Dalefoot	BRADFORD	BD21 4SE	Accounts	~~D~~ B	May	00182	R416 PAM
Charnock	Alicia	10 Westgate	Well Bank	BRADFORD	BD17 3LW	Sales	D	Aug	01028	N703 9UA
Clare	Alison	Dale Head	Burn Wood	BRADFORD	BD19 7DH	Personnel	A	Aug	00201	R104 ALI
Dale	Colin	1 Cromwell Drive	Farringdon	BRADFORD	BD5 4NS	~~Purchasing~~ Accounts	E	July	01029	M42 DCA
Fielden	Jonathan	5 South Parade	Whitfield	LEEDS	LS23 7NP	Accounts	D	July	00437	—
Fitzgerald	Sonya	~~1 Field Side~~ ~~16 Arncliffe Lane~~	Dalefoot	BRADFORD	BD21 2LD	Marketing	B	Aug	01210	P774 DBL
Gannon	Kathleen	8 Lea Grove	Well Bank	BRADFORD	BD17 7JS	Sales	E	Mar	00876	—
Hartley	Shirley	16 Sandhall Road	Well Bank	BRADFORD	BD17 2RA	Sales	D	July	01024	K173 WEL
James	Iain	131 Lodge Grove	Stonemount	BRADFORD	BD10 9RA	Marketing	E	June	00997	K714 NUJ
Khalid	Mukhtar	13 South Parade	Whitfield	LEEDS	LS23 7PR	Sales	B	~~Oct~~ Aug	00434	N494 PRM
Khan	Sofina	13 Whalley Road	Eastfield	LEEDS	LS10 4WA	Production	D	July	00682	—
Lawrence	Sarah ~~Katie~~ Katie	Highcroft	Burn Wood	BRADFORD	BD19 3AL	Purchasing	D	April	00449	L490 REN
Lewis	Kay	Howard Hall	Dalefoot	BRADFORD	BD21 5RT	Production	B	Sept	00236	R632 KTL
~~Lobode~~	~~Francis~~	~~17 Moorend Grove~~	~~Whitfield~~	~~LEEDS~~	~~LS23 5SL~~	~~Production~~	~~D~~	~~Aug~~	~~01023~~ (To be deleted)	
Morris	Graham	60 Sherby Drive	Dalefoot	BRADFORD	BD21 5LV	Production	A	Mar	00144	P447 DUC
Petrovic	Tadeusz	Green House	Hallenshaw	BRADFORD	BD16 2EN	Purchasing	C	April	00132	P703 TED
Reed	Adam	8 Grange Road	Stonemount	BRADFORD	BD10 1NS	Sales	C	Feb	00672	L101 ADR
Roche	Sandra	37 Denfield ~~Grove~~ Lane	Farringdon	BRADFORD	BD5 5NQ	Sales	B	Aug	01021	N204 AND

LastName	FirstName	Address1	Address2	City	PostalCode	Dept	Grade	Appraisal	Payroll	Car Reg
Roper	Jim	Hill Crest	Hallenshaw	BRADFORD	BD16 3RF	Accounts	D	July	01022	M721 PER
Sawyer	Kevin	17 Badger Lane	Hollins	LEEDS	LS3 6HB	Marketing	B	Jan	00642	M462 KEL
Shuvla ~~Miss Milos~~		14 Cook Street	Eastfield	LEEDS	LS10 4EA	Production	D	July	00239	—
Southgate	Daniel	11 George Street	Whitfield	LEEDS	LS23 1TV	Production	D	July	00592	—
Sykes	William	2 Oliver's Way	Arden	LEEDS	LS6 8RD	Production	B	Dec	00690	P68 ROD
~~Sykes~~	~~Valerie~~	~~2 Oliver's Way~~	~~Arden~~	~~LEEDS~~	~~LS6 8RD~~	~~Sales~~	~~D~~	~~July~~	~~00691~~	(to be deleted)
Woodhead	Steven	4 Woodview Avenue	Well Bank	BRADFORD	BD17 7LA	Production	C	Jan	00668	M175 SWH
Woodhead	Lee	52 Wakefield Road	Farringdon	BRADFORD	BD5 2DB	Production	D	July	00789	—
Zimmer	Marc	4 Woodhouse Road	Burn Wood	BRADFORD	BD19 9SH	Production	E̶ D	Dec	00671	—
Stewart	Vikki	6 Vale Rd	Hollins	LEEDS	LS10 4ES	Sales	C	Aug	01030	P996 LEM
Challoner	Amy	3 Bailey Gro	Dalefoot	BFD	BD21 5RT	Marketing	D	Aug	01031	K311 LEA
Riva	Rachel	20 Bank St	Roundhill	BFD	BD7 5LS	Production	E	Sept	01032	—
Rowan	Paul	721 Leeds Rd	Farringdon	BFD	BD5 6NQ	Production	B	Sept	01033	R333 WAN
Simha	Sohan	70 Cliffe View	Arden	LDS	LS6 6TF	Sales	D	Sept	01034	—
Hussain	Leyla	34 Lister Dr	Burnwood	BFD	BD19 9HJ	Purchasing	C	Sept	01035	N196 UJX
Philpott	Michael	Spring House	Hallenshaw	BFD	BD16 2RL	Marketing	A	Aug	01036	P970 MPT
Weir	Sharon	18 Duke's Sq	Whitfield	LDS	LS23 7NO	Accounts	C	Sept	01037	J665 WXY
Anwar	Salome	10 Cliffe Ave	Arden	LDS	LS6 6TP	Personnel	B	Aug	01038	N383 MSM
Woolf	Anya	7 Crag End	Dalefoot	BFD	BD21 6XW	Sales	B	Aug	01039	N214 ASA
Zaleski	Mario	5 Moor Grove	Eastfield	LDS	LS10 5OM	Production	D	Sept	01040	—
Moorby	Derek	Hazel Garth	Arden	LDS	LS6 8RD	Production	B	Aug	01041	P68 RED
Maud	Rita	6 Broadway	Stonemount	BFD	BD10 6AW	Production	C	Aug	01042	L884 TAL
Duncan	Matthew	10 Chapel Rd	Farringdon	BFD	BD5 8PA	Sales	E	Aug	01043	J611 RND
Byrne	Sean	55 Anne's Way	Arden	LDS	LS6 5AA	Accounts	D	Aug	01044	—

Please put BRADFORD and LEEDS in full throughout

Key in the following records to create a datafile for use with Document 4. Save as UNIT15DATA2 and print one copy.

Mrs H A Bulmer
16 Southmead Lane
NORCHESTER
NR6 4SE
Cat

Ms R S West
Arran View
HARRISTON
HN3 8TN
Cat

Mr L Halls
Rose Cottage
GLENDALE
GE10 3SG
Dog

Mrs J Harr
11 Sandy Road
GLENDALE
GE9 9SJ
Cat

Ms M E Kallo
10 Surrey Street
NORCHESTER
NR4 3RS
Dog

Mrs A M Smith
33 Queens Rd
NORCHESTER
NR8 3MA
Dog

Mrs B Fyffe
3 Leyland Grove
GLENDALE
GE3 7DN
Dog

Ms J Christie
136 Union St
NORCHESTER
NR2 2NL
Dog

Mr L G Mann .
62 Borough Rd West
NORCHESTER
NR1 1HR
Dog

Mr F R Ciccone
11 Higher Falls
HARRISTON
HN6 4RF
Cat

Please key in this memo to be merged with UNIT15DATA1. Insert merge codes as shown and use a justified right margin. Print one copy of the standard document and memos to all staff members living in Dalefoot.

MEMO

To: *FirstName *LastName, *Dept Department
From: Tessa McLoughlin, Operations Manager
Ref: TM/OM/*Payroll

STAFF CAR PARKING

Redevelopment work on the Company's car parking facilities is almost completed. The new car park to the east of the site will be opened at the end of this month.

Staff travelling from Leeds are recommended to use the A580 and then Parkwood Road for ease of access (see attached map).

Passes will be issued over the next two weeks. Our records show the following car as registered in your name:

Vehicle Registration No: *Car Reg

Please inform me if you have changed your vehicle or if you would like to register a second vehicle.

Enc

Please key in the following standard document to merge with the datafile created in Document 2. Insert merge codes where indicated by * and use an unjustified right margin. Print one copy of the standard document and also print documents to all enquirers from Norchester who own a dog.

Ref: JR/PetIns/NORCHESTER

* Title * Initials *Surname
* Street
* Town
* Postcode

Dear * Title. * Surname

LOOKING AFTER YOUR BEST FRIEND ←—— (emphasise)

Thank you for your recent enquiry regarding insurance for family pets. As a caring pet owner, you want to make sure that your * Pet gets the best treatment in case of injury or illness. Unfortunately, approximately one third of pets require veterinary treatment each year, and the fees can be a worry.

ACE Pet Insurance can give you peace of mind at a low cost. Cover can be individually tailored to suit your pet and can be extended to include holiday cancellation, theft, straying and death. Full details are enclosed.

For a free quotation and immediate cover, please ring our Hotline on 0115 254 3383. Alternatively, come along to meet our specially qualified staff at the Norchester Veterinary Centre on Wednesday 24 August between 6 pm and 9 pm. You will find that you can put your mind at rest for a small charge.

Yrs sincerely

J Russell
Pet Insurance Manager

Enc

Unit	Topic	Date completed	Comments
► 1	Proofreading text		
	Typographical and spelling errors		
	Spelling and grammar check		
	AutoCorrect		
	Formatting/emphasising text		
	Margin alignment		
	Line spacing		
	Changing margin settings		
	Changing the typing line length		
► 2	Grammatical and punctuation errors and abbreviations		
	Correction signs		
	Adding text to a document at a later time		
	Page numbering continuation sheets – page breaks		
	Characters not available on keyboard		
	Consistency of presentation		
► 3	Business letter layout		
	Special marks and enclosure marks		
	Pre-printed forms and templates		
	Memorandum layout		
	Automatic date Insertion		
	Locating information from another document – confirming facts		
► 4	Consolidation 1		
► 5	Examination Practice 1 – RSA Stage II Text Processing Part 1		
► 6	Changing the typing line length, indent text, inset margins		
	Re-arranging text		
	Find and replace text		
	Headers and footers		
	Allocate space		
	Sort facility		
► 7	Tables		
	Sub-divided and multi-line headings		
	Moving sections in a table		
	Sorting text in a table		

▶ 8	Standard Paragraphs		
	Creating standard paragraphs/phrases		
	Inserting standard paragraphs/phrases		
▶ 9	Routing business documents		
	Indicating routing and printing copies		
	Enumeration		
	Producing letters and memos using standard paragraphs/phrases		
	Producing letters and memos using pre-printed forms and templates		
▶ 10	Consolidation 2		
▶ 11	Examination Practice 2 – RSA Stage II Word Processing Part 2		
▶ 12	Mailmerge – Main document		
	Create a datafile		
	Add, delete and amend records		
	Merge main document and data file		
	Print merged documents		
▶ 13	Mailmerge – add and delete fields		
	Sort datafile		
	Select records		
	Merge main document and selected records		
	Print merged records		
▶ 14	Consolidation 3		
▶ 15	Examination Practice 3 – RSA Stage II Mailmerge Part 2		

Print-out checks

Unit 1
Exercise 1D

ADVERTISEMENT FOR LODGINGS

In reply to the recent advertisement for temporary board and lodgings for visiting company representatives, I am able to recommend a small but friendly Guest House close to the town centre. Several of my own business clients have used this accommodation before and have experienced it to be more than satisfactory.

Most of the bedrooms come with a separate bathroom and I believe there is ample access to car parking facilities. The owner is a very responsible lady who offers an extremely flexible service, particularly with meal arrangements. Apparently, the prices are also very reasonable but it may be worth requesting a definite up-to-date of room types and financial details.

Any further correspondence should be addressed to:

Mrs Jean Mayberry
Mayberry House
Thorne Lane
BURNLEY BL2 4EU

Unit 1
Exercise 1C

ADVERTISEMENT FOR LODGINGS

In reply to the recent advertisements for temporary board and lodgings for visiting company representatives, I am able to recommend a small but friendly Guest House close to the town centre. Several of my own business clients have used this accommodation before and have experienced it to be more than satisfactory.

Most of the bedrooms come with a separate bathroom and I believe there is ample access to car parking facilities. The owner is a very responsible lady who offers an extremely flexible service, particularly with meal arrangements. Apparently, the prices are also very reasonable but it may be worth requesting a definite up-to-date of room types and financial details.

Any further correspondence should be addressed to:

Mrs Jean Mayberry
Mayberry House
Thorne Lane
BURNLEY BL2 4EU

ACE BUSINESS SERVICES

MEMORANDUM

LEADERSHIP STYLES

Autocratic

Behavioural style of leaders who tend to impose decisions rather than discuss them, work separately from the group and dictate work methods. They often limit colleague's access to information and knowledge about goals to just the next step to be performed, and sometimes give feedback that is punitive through formal processes.

Laissez-faire

Behavioural style of leaders who prefer others to take the lead in being responsible and will recommend self-direction. They usually believe in handing over complete freedom to the group, provide sufficient and necessary materials, respond only when answering questions and avoid giving feedback.

It has been suggested that the apparent lack of

concern in a laissez-faire leader has a worse effect

on business working relationships than that of an

autocratic leader!

Democratic

Behavioural style of leaders who generally acknowledge a high level of motivation in others and tend to involve the group in decision making. They appreciate contributions and encourage groups to develop their own work methods, convey overall goals to be achieved, and use the feedback as an opportunity and useful experience for helpful coaching.

ACE BUSINESS SERVICES

246 Park View
LEEDS LS1 6RD

Tel no: 0113 246589   Fax no: 0113 246577

<u>CUSTOMER INFORMATION</u>

PLACING AN ORDER

It is our intention to achieve our target of supplying all of our customers with all of the goods ordered on the date promised. You can help us to help you by preparing your order before telephoning. If you need further information on any of our products, we recommend that you refer to our company's Customer Information Service. We can give an immediate response to most queries. If necessary, we will check details with manufacturers and call you back within approximately 2 to 3 hours.

<u>By telephone</u>

Ring our Order Hotline number when you have prepared a list of your needs. Our operator will ask you for the following information: catalogue number, colour or size, description, price per unit, quantity, customer number. If our lines are busy, you will be asked to leave your customer number and telephone number. We will call you back as soon as we possibly can.

<u>By fax</u>

If you have access to a fax machine, we would be pleased to receive your order in this way to save you time and money. We supply order forms in the form of a pad printed to ensure no details are omitted.

Please do remember to tell us if you require delivery to an address which is different to the one registered on our customer database and which is normally used for all correspondence.

If you need to contact us after office hours, our answerphone will record your message and/or your order.

<u>Terms</u>

Pre-paid by 1 week or cash on delivery. Bank or trade references will take about 10 days; after this clearance time we will accept cheques. Returned or re-presented cheques will be charged at £15 on each occasion.

We reserve the right not to accept orders, and all goods remain our property until they have been paid for.

Your signature on delivery acknowledges receipt of all the goods shown on the invoice at the price given and in good condition. Claims can be accepted only on concerns regarding quality. Contact the Customer Information Service in the unlikely event of such a problem. We will do our best to resolve the issue to your satisfaction.

<u>Delivery</u>

Refer to our map (on separate page at front of catalogue) to determine the day of the week when deliveries are made to your area. The minimum order amount is shown on this page. We feel sure you will appreciate that an order must be sufficiently large to justify **free delivery**.

2

<u>CUSTOMER INFORMATION</u>

PLACING ORDERS

It is our intention to achieve our target of supplying all of our customers with all of the goods ordered on the date promised. You can help us to help you by preparing your order before telephoning.

If you **need** further information on any of our products, we recommend that you refer to our company's Customer Information Service. We can give an immediate response to most queries. If necessary, we will check details with manufacturers and call you back within approximately 2 to 3 hours.

<u>By telephone</u>

Ring our Order Hotline number when you have prepared a list of your requirements. Our operator will ask you for the following information: catalogue number, colour or size, description, quantity, price per unit, customer number.

If our lines are busy, you will be asked to leave your customer number and telephone number. We will call you back as soon as we possibly can. This means that you will not be wasting valuable time.

<u>By fax</u>

If you have access to a fax machine, we would be pleased to receive your order in this way to save you time and money. We supply order forms in the form of a printed pad to ensure no details are omitted. Please do remember to tell us if you require delivery to an address which is different to the one registered on our customer database and which is normally used for all correspondence.

If you need to contact us after office hours, 9.00 am to 5.30 pm Monday to Friday, our answerphone will record your message and/or your order.

1

RENTINET

YOUR GATEWAY TO THE WORLD

For just £14.00 (+ VAT) per month plus an initial payment of only £25.00 (+ VAT), you can be instantly connected to the rest of the world!

With over 30 million users world-wide, the Internet is growing at an unbelievable 12% per month. Realise the potential for your organisation!

Let us take all the worry out of your technological information and communications systems.

SETTING-UP PACKAGE (£25.00 + VAT at 17.5 % = £ 29.38)

Sign-up registration charge
Set-up of Internet account
Configuration of computer and modem
Fully-licensed software

Save 10 % if you pay for 1 year in advance - £22.00 saving!

SYSTEM CHECK

Your IBM-compatible PC will need:

Windows 3.1	4 Mb RAM	5 Mb free hard disk space
Windows 95	8 Mb RAM	20 Mb free hard disk space
Apple Macintosh	8 Mb RAM	5 Mb free hard disk space

MEMORANDUM

To: Elisabeth Händel, Advertising Unit

From: Adèle Mélin, Marketing Unit

Date: Date of typing

RENTINET Centre

As discussed earlier today, I enclose hard copy for use in designing the flyers for the launch of the above Centre. I also enclose the text on disk to save time.

Please let me have the drafts for checking in the following formats so that I can decide on the most effective size and cost:

A5	149 mm x 210 mm	80 gsm	écru
A4	210 mm x 297 mm	100 gsm	orange

As there are only 3½ weeks to go until the Centre launch I would appreciate it if you could give this matter your urgent attention. I look forward to seeing your design ideas and a range of suitable graphics as soon as possible.

Encs

RENTINET

YOUR GATEWAY TO THE WORLD

For just £14.00 (+ VAT) per month plus an initial payment of only £25.00 (+ VAT), you can be instantly connected to the rest of the world!

With over 30 million users world-wide, the Internet is growing at an unbelievable 12% per month. Realise the potential for your organisation!

Let us take all the worry out of your technological information and communications systems.

SETTING-UP PACKAGE (£25.00 + VAT at 17.5 % = £ 29.38)

Sign-up registration charge
Set-up of Internet account
Configuration of computer and modem
Fully-licensed software

Save 10 % if you pay for 1 year in advance - £22.00 saving!

The RENTINET Centre is open for Setting-up from
9.00 am to 6.00 pm   Monday to Thursday
9.00 am to 8.00 pm   Friday to Saturday

Just bring along your PC – we'll do the rest.
(Booking advised – Tel: Matthias Schneider on 01234-1098765)

We realise you may not be able to leave the office – we'll come to you. FREE setting-up session within 8 mile radius. £15.00 fee for 9 to 15 miles radius

We realise you may need help – the RENTINET Centre will be your local advice point – always there when you need us.

Still teetering on the brink? Take the plunge. RENTINET is your guarantee of a safe landing!

SYSTEM CHECK

Your IBM compatible PC will need:

Windows 3.1	4 Mb RAM	5 Mb free hard disk space
Windows 95	8 Mb RAM	20 Mb free hard disk space
Apple Macintosh	8 Mb RAM	5 Mb free hard disk space

ACE BUSINESS SERVICES

246 Park View
LEEDS LS1 6RD

Tel no: 0113 246589   Fax no: 0113 246577

Our ref: SM/24P

Today's date

FOR THE ATTENTION OF BRIAN WADSWORTH

Décor-8
36 Newberry Avenue
LEEDS
LS2 3TW

Dear Sirs

We were very pleased with the decorating work which you carried out last year on our conference suite. In acknowledgement of this, we wish to advise you that there will be an opportunity in the near future for you to tender for work to be undertaken in our new training unit.

I will be inviting several firms to inspect the premises and provide us with an estimate for the costs for decorating this new accommodation. There will also be an opportunity for you to meet my colleague, Deborah Pickles, who is our Training Manager and who will provide you with more information about our requirements.

I expect to hold a meeting at the beginning of next month and would be grateful if you could confirm the dates when you would be available on the enclosed reply slip.

Yours faithfully

Steven Murgatroyd
ASSISTANT PREMISES OFFICER

Enc

ACE BUSINESS SERVICES

MEMORANDUM

From: Deborah Pickles, Training Manager
To: Steven Murgatroyd, Assistant Premises Officer
Ref: SM/864
Date: today's

I am writing with reference to our recent discussions relating to the proposal for a new company training unit to be housed in the old staff lounge. The steering committee has prepared a report on the details and a copy is attached.

I would appreciate it if you could prepare a separate estimate of the expenses that are likely to be incurred for the unit's refurbishment inclusive of all decorations, fixtures and fittings, along with any necessary structural alterations.

This information is required by Friday (date of Friday of next week), or sooner if possible.

We will, of course, need to obtain proper tenders for the work to be done from reputable organisations. I understand you have already begun to contact some of the local firms who have been recommended to us in the past. With regard to the fixtures and fittings, I attach a list of manufacturers with whom we hold accounts for you to contact.

Encs

ACE BUSINESS SERVICES

246 Park View
LEEDS LS1 6RD

Tel no: 0113 246589   Fax no: 0113 246577

Today's date

URGENT

Mr Brian Shaw
Strand Furniture Supplies
3 Merton Road
BRADFORD
BD17 4RW

Dear Mr Shaw

I have recently received a brochure of your range of office furniture. As we are refurbishing the company's new training unit I wonder if it would be possible for me to visit your premises in order to view the different ranges more closely and to inspect the quality and appearance.

I will need your assurance that any items ordered would be delivered within the next eight weeks.

Also, you do not indicate in your correspondence whether discounts would be available for large orders, or the time period for any extended guarantee.

Perhaps you could contact my secretary, Marjorie Wallace, to arrange a suitable time for me to visit your company, preferably within the next two weeks. Marjorie's telephone extension number is 237. It would be helpful, in the meantime, if you could forward some fabric samples from your standard range of office chairs in the pre-paid envelope enclosed.

I look forward to hearing from you in the near future.

Yours sincerely

Deborah Pickles
TRAINING MANAGER

Enc

ACE BUSINESS SERVICES

246 Park View
LEEDS LS1 6RD

Tel no: 0113 246589   Fax no: 0113 246577

Our ref: TR/437/pn

Your ref: 1791/32BR

Today's date

FOR THE ATTENTION OF ABDUL AZIZ

Mace Bothers Ltd
Leverton Business Park
SHIPLEY
SH4 9TW

Dear Sirs

As you are one of our most valued clients, I was very pleased to hear that several members of staff from your organisation will be able to attend our Special Promotions event next month. I attach a map showing directions of how to get to the venue and also an agenda for the afternoon.

There will be an opportunity to discuss any special requirements you may have with the personnel responsible for each specialist area of work. In particular, I believe you will be interested in meeting the staff from our Foreign Affairs department who have significant experience in developing opportunities for overseas export and trade.

May I also recommend that you spend some time with our Marketing Director, David Jamieson, who has assisted your company on a number of previous occasions. David has developed some new methods of producing eye-catching advertisements that could be of benefit to your own future publicity campaigns.

Yours faithfully

Terence Irvine
GENERAL MANAGER

Encs

ACE BUSINESS SERVICES

MEMORANDUM

From: Steven Murgatroyd, Assistant Premises Officer
To: Deborah Pickles, Training Manager
Ref: DP/33RT
Date: today's

REFURBISHMENT OF THE NEW TRAINING UNIT

With regard to your recent memo concerning the above, please find attached my estimate for complete refurbishment of the new unit, inclusive of decorations, furniture and miscellaneous items. Although you did not specifically request it, I have also included the approximate cost of additional technology requirements such as telephone lines, computer cabling and access points etc.

There are several different ranges of furniture within the price bracket listed. The final choice is largely a matter of personal preference and I enclose several catalogues for you to look through.

Apparently, no major structural alterations are necessary although I would recommend that any financial savings in this area be re-allocated to improving the nearby cloakroom facilities.

I have invited several decorating contractors to meet with you. In particular I can recommend a firm called Décor-8 who have previously undertaken work for us of a high standard. Their contact name is Brian Wadsworth.

A list of alternative dates is appended. If these dates are inconvenient I would appreciate it if you could notify me immediately.

Encs

Unit 4
Exercise 4B

ACE BUSINESS SERVICES

MEMORANDUM

From: Terence Irvine, General Manager
To: David Jamieson, Marketing Director
Ref: TI/396
Date: today's

SPECIAL PROMOTIONS EVENT

With reference to the above event to be held next month, I have circulated letters to some of our major clients who may be interested in attending.

I recall that you have previously done some work with one company in particular, namely Mace Brothers Ltd, and wonder if you could follow up my letter with a personal call.

As I have highlighted the inclusion of our Foreign Affairs department, I would appreciate it if you could ensure that we have extra publicity stands and literature available that will provide sufficient information about all aspects of its work.

I think it's essential that we have a general meeting several days before the event to ensure that all members of staff are aware of their individual responsibilities. Will you take the necessary steps to convene the meeting?

Please let me know if there's anything further that you wish to discuss in relation to the event.

Unit 4
Exercise 4C

OUR FUTURE ON THE WORLD WIDE WEB

It is said that the Internet is one of the most significant developments of our time. The Net stretches around the globe like an electronic spider's web, interweaving communication links so that people from all parts of the world connect in one massive computerised society.

Analysts have theorised about the possible future implications of the Internet. People will expect to be connected to the Net wherever they are - on a plane, in a car, on a bicycle or in their living rooms. Already, Internet telephones are hot products in the marketplace. Some feel that disconnection and privacy will become two of the most treasured qualities of the 21st century.

The speed at which the Net is developing is faster than any technological change ever seen before.

Net Opinions

There are currently two main schools of extreme opinion about the wider impacts of the Internet on society.

To the left there is the 'wired community' which views the Net as uncontrollable and advocates that this giant global network joining ordinary people cannot be managed or restrained by any State or corporation.

By its nature it is subversive and it will bring an end to many traditional notions of Western-style economics such as taxation, national currencies and national borders. National frontiers will continue to shrink as we become inhabitants of the 'Virtual Society' or cyberspace. It also means an end to our concepts of intellectual property copyright.

To the right there are politicians, regulators and governments who seek to control the Web. Censorship is a topic frequently highlighted by the media as they unveil the ever-increasing amount of 'porn' freely available on-line. Right-wingers often find themselves caught between the desire to have a high-tech infrastructure for their economies and the fear that an uncontrollable universal network might prove extremely subversive.

Occupying the middle ground are those who understand the issues but believe that the 'worst-case' scenarios are unlikely. Optimism arises from the belief that today's hype about the Information Superhighway will be tomorrow's understatement.

1

Unit 4
Exercise 4C continued

Net Growth

It is envisaged that by the turn of the millennium there will be approximately half a

billion users linked to the Net, including almost every business, organisation,

government authority, school and individual professional or entrepreneur.

The Era of the World Wide Web

We are entering a new era in which our economies and social fabrics will be shaped by the world's public and private data networks.

National economic boundaries, already blurred by the use of private financial dealing networks, will cease to exist in a few years and companies (and countries) large and small, will have to re-engineer the way they conduct their business. This presents a significant challenge for tomorrow's business managers.

Although it may be relatively easy to grasp the idea of connecting the world's computers together over the telephone lines, it may be more difficult to fully realise just how much our lives will change as a result of such a simple concept.

Unit 5
Exercise 5A

ACE BUSINESS SERVICES
246 Park View
LEEDS LS1 6RD

Tel no: 0113 246589   Fax no: 0113 246577

Today's date

PERSONAL

Mrs Sarah Phelps
63 The Poplars
Kirkbride Crescent
SKIPTON
BD25 1PB

Dear Mrs Phelps

With reference to your recent enquiry regarding possible vacancies in our Sales Department, please find enclosed an application form on which you may provide us with the information we need in order to assess your experience and suitability for such a post. You may return this to us, complete with your signature, in the envelope provided.

Please note that we will require at least two references, one of which should be from your previous employer. If you wish, you may also include an up-to-date C.V. with the application form.

Although we do not have any immediate vacancies, I believe there will be an opportunity to apply for several permanent positions in approximately three months' time. In the meantime, our Sales Manager, Mr Mila Yokovic, has informed me that he is considering the possibility of recruiting for a temporary post in the interim period. I have passed your details to Mr Yokovic so that he can contact you direct.

Thank you for your interest in our company.

Yours sincerely

Gabrielle Macpherson
PERSONNEL MANAGER

Encs

2

UNDERSTANDING ORGANISATIONS THROUGH METAPHORS

THE NOTION OF METAPHORS

Metaphors are used essentially as a way of implying a hidden meaning through the use of words, or a figure of speech, which conjure up a particular image in the mind.

Our thoughts are generally communicated to others through the language of written or spoken words. It has been said that a man's language is an index of his mind. Thus, the manner in which language is used can be seen as a mirror of the thought-processes that initiated it.

THE USE OF METAPHORS

The use of linguistic metaphors draws attention to specific resemblance between different situations or experiences in order to highlight distinctive similarities. Take, for instance, the expression 'My head is like a spinning top!' By using a familiar figure of speech the speaker is able to personify the hidden state of mind he/she is feeling.

The particular metaphor singled out for use, however, can be used to force a particular viewpoint to the front and push other viewpoints to the rear (if not concealing them altogether).

To illustrate, extreme chauvinists have been quoted as saying that 'women have butterfly minds' - the implication here is that women lack sufficient concentration to produce effective results and the metaphor is used to personify a negative quality in women. In a similar context, but using a different metaphor, it has been said that 'men use helicopter planning procedures'. Although both figures of speech convey a similar concept of 'flitting from one thing to another', the choice of metaphor alludes to a quite distinct, and opposite, meaning.

The metaphorical play on words to allege a particular idea or concept can even be applied to the same word used in a different context. Take, for instance, the word 'giant'. When we describe a certain individual as being like a gentle giant the metaphorical description implies a kind of clumsy docility. On the other hand, when Armstrong walked on the moon's surface, it was said that this was a giant step for mankind. In the latter example, the metaphorical use of the same key word, giant, implies heroism and victory.

1

ACE BUSINESS SERVICES

MEMORANDUM

FROM: Gabrielle Macpherson, Personnel Manager
TO: Mila Yokovic, Sales Manager
REF: GM/382
DATE: today's

As discussed with you on the telephone earlier, I have received an enquiry in relation to possible vacancies in the Sales Department. I have advised the applicant of the likelihood of the forthcoming permanent vacancies and also the temporary vacancy for which you were going to place an advertisement.

I recommend that you contact the applicant direct in regard to the latter vacancy. As she is quite experienced in sales I believe you may be interested in meeting her. The applicant's name is Mrs Sarah Phelps. Her address is 63 The Poplars, Kirkbride Crescent, SKIPTON, BD25 1PB. I have already forwarded the necessary correspondence to her for completion. Can you let me know the outcome?

Apparently, I have not yet been provided with the criteria for the new sales positions. I appreciate your heavy workload at this time of the year but I am sure you will agree it is necessary for you to provide sufficient information to ensure that the job descriptions are relevant to your current needs.

<u>CUSTOMER INFORMATION</u>

PLACING ORDERS

It is our intention to achieve our target of supplying all of our customers with all of the goods ordered on the date promised. You can help us to help you by preparing your order before telephoning.

If you need further information on any of our products, we recommend that you refer to our company's Customer Information Service. We can give an immediate response to most queries. If necessary, we will check details with manufacturers and call you back within approximately 2 to 3 hours.

By telephone

Ring our Order Hotline number when you have prepared a list of your requirements. Our operator will ask you for the following information: catalogue number, colour or size, description, quantity, price per unit, customer number.

If our lines are busy, you will be asked to leave your customer number and telephone number. We will call you back as soon as we possibly can. This means that you will not be wasting valuable time.

By fax

If you have access to a fax machine, we would be pleased to receive your order in this way to save you time and money. We supply order forms in the form of a printed pad to ensure no details are omitted. Please do remember to tell us if you require delivery to an address which is different to the one registered on our customer database and which is normally used for all correspondence.

If you need to contact us after office hours, 9.00 am to 5.30 pm Monday to Friday, our answerphone will record your message and/or your order.

1

METAPHORS AND ORGANISATIONS

Theorists often argue that many of our ideas about organisations are metaphorical, with a number of common images being used to demonstrate resemblance.

Managers who see organisations as MACHINES often lose sight of the human factors, organising situations in a more mechanistic way with people making up the interlocking parts of the machine to keep it functioning as a whole. The expression 'I feel just like a spare part' is, perhaps, an expression which may be heard when the organisational culture places greater emphasis on the smooth running of the mechanism than the needs of the operatives.

Organisations are sometimes referred to as if they were ORGANISMS which can be born, grow, develop, or die as if somehow the organisation is a living thing able to respond and adapt to a changing environment and develop its own evolutionary pattern.

Some managers see organisations as BRAINS. Phrases such as 'learning organisation' and 'brainchild of' draw attention to information processing, learning and intelligence. It is as if the organisation can analyse situations, learn from its mistakes and reason on the way forward.

The key factor in the effective use of metaphors is to build on them, to deliberately adopt a number of alternative viewpoints that may reflect organisational life. Developing such a multi-faceted approach will provide a broader focus for improving strategic decisions.

Reading organisations through metaphors focuses attention on different aspects and general principles of organisational structure and behaviour - the way an organisation interacts with its environment, views its workforce, operates decision making, defines strategies, distributes power, selects and promotes its management, and controls (or not) its management hierarchy.

Conceptualisation is coloured in the way in which a metaphor is applied.

2

SUPERNET

<u>YOUR GATEWAY TO THE WORLD</u>

For just £14.00 (+ VAT) per month plus an initial payment of only £25.00 (+ VAT), you can be instantly connected to the rest of the world! With over 30 million users world-wide, the Internet is growing at an unbelievable 12% per month. Realise the potential for your organisation!

We realise you may need help – the SUPERNET Centre will be your <u>local</u> advice point – always there when you need us.

Let us take all the worry out of your technological information and communications systems.

<u>SETTING-UP PACKAGE</u> (£25.00 + VAT at 17.5 % = £ 29.38)

Configuration of computer and modem
Sign-up registration charge
Set-up of Internet account
Fully-licensed software

Save 10 % if you pay for 1 year in advance - £22.00 saving!

The SUPERNET Centre is open for Setting-up from
9.00 am to 6.00 pm   Monday to Thursday
9.00 am to 8.00 pm   Friday to Saturday
10.00 am to 4.00 pm   Sunday

Just bring along your PC – we'll do the rest.
(Booking advised – Tel: Matthias Schneider or James Hall on 01234-1098765)

We realise you may not be able to leave the office – we'll come to you. FREE setting-up session within 8 mile radius. £15.00 fee for 9 to 15 miles radius

<u>SYSTEM CHECK</u>

Your IBM compatible PC will need:

Windows 3.1	4 Mb RAM	5 Mb free hard disk space
Windows 95	8 Mb RAM	20 Mb free hard disk space
Apple Macintosh	8 Mb RAM	5 Mb free hard disk space

Still teetering on the brink? Take the plunge. SUPERNET is your guarantee of a safe landing!

1

<u>Terms</u>

Pre-paid by 1 week or cash on delivery. Bank or trade references will take about 10 days; after this clearance time we will accept cheques. Returned or re-presented cheques will be charged at £15 on each occasion.

We reserve the right not to accept orders, and all goods remain our property until they have been paid for.

Your signature on delivery acknowledges receipt of all the goods shown on the invoice at the price given and in good condition. Claims can be accepted only on concerns regarding quality. Contact the Customer Information Service in the unlikely event of such a problem. We will do our best to resolve the issue to your satisfaction.

<u>Delivery</u>

Refer to our map (on separate page at front of catalogue) to determine the day of the week when deliveries are made to your area. The minimum order amount is shown on this page. We feel sure you will appreciate that an order must be sufficiently large to justify **free delivery.**

2

Unit 6
Exercise 6C

Your name   Exercise 6C   RSA Centre No

CUSTOMER INFORMATION

PLACING ORDERS

It is our intention to achieve our target of supplying all of our customers with all of the goods ordered on the date promised. You can help us to help you by preparing your order before telephoning.

If you need further information on any of our products, we recommend that you refer to our company's Customer Information Service. We can give an immediate response to most queries. If necessary, we will check details with manufacturers and call you back within approximately 2 to 3 hours.

By telephone

Ring our Order Hotline number when you have prepared a list of your requirements. Our operator will ask you for the following information: catalogue number, colour or size, description, quantity, price per unit, customer number.

If our lines are busy, you will be asked to leave your customer number and telephone number. We will call you back as soon as we possibly can. This means that you will not be wasting valuable time.

By fax

If you have access to a fax machine, we would be pleased to receive your order in this way to save you time and money. We supply order forms in the form of a printed pad to ensure no details are omitted. Please do remember to tell us if you require delivery to an address which is different to the one registered on our customer database and which is normally used for all correspondence.

If you need to contact us after office hours, 9.00 am to 5.30 pm Monday to Friday, our answerphone will record your message and/or your order.

1

Unit 6
Exercise 6B continued

Whether you are a small business user or you use a computer at home for study and general interest, we can offer you expert help. Our specialist technicians are well trained and they speak your language. We won't confuse you with unnecessary jargon – just tell us what you want from your computer and we'll tell you how to get started.

Many of our recent customers, who were new to computer use are now happily using E-mail to communicate with friends and colleagues for business or pleasure.

Students of all ages can enjoy access to an endless source of information in the form of text and graphics.

Business users can be sure that the information in their reports is up-to-date and relevant.

Anyone who has an interest or hobby can communicate with others of a like mind through a News group.

OPEN 7 DAYS – ALWAYS THERE WHEN YOU NEED US

WHY WAIT – JOIN THE INTERNET CROWD TODAY!

SUPERNET TEL 01234-1098765

Let us take all the worry out of your technological information and communications systems.

2

Your name   Exercise 6C   RSA Centre No

Terms

Pre-paid by 1 week or cash on delivery. Bank or trade references will take about 10 days, after this clearance time we will accept cheques. Returned or re-presented cheques will be charged at £15 on each occasion.

We reserve the right not to accept orders, and all goods remain our property until they have been paid for.

Your signature on delivery acknowledges receipt of all the goods shown on the invoice at the price given and in good condition. Claims can be accepted only on concerns regarding quality. Contact the Customer Information Service in the unlikely event of such a problem. We will do our best to resolve the issue to your satisfaction.

Delivery

Refer to our map (on separate page at front of catalogue) to determine the day of the week when deliveries are made to your area. The minimum order amount is shown on this page. We feel sure you will appreciate that an order must be sufficiently large to justify **free delivery**.

2

Your name   Exercise 6D   RSA Centre No

PLACING ORDERS

It is our intention to achieve our target of supplying all of our clients with all of the goods ordered on the date promised. You can help us to help you by preparing your order before telephoning.

By fax

If you have access to a fax machine, we would be pleased to receive your order in this way to save you time and money. We supply order forms in the form of a printed pad to ensure no details are omitted. Please do remember to tell us if you require delivery to an address which is different to the one registered on our client database and which is normally used for all correspondence.

By telephone

Ring our Order Hotline number when you have prepared a list of your requirements. Our operator will ask you for the following information: catalogue number, colour or size, description, quantity, price per unit, client number.

If our lines are busy, you will be asked to leave your client number and telephone number. We will call you back as soon as we possibly can. This means that you will not be wasting valuable time.

If you need to contact us after office hours, 9.00 am to 5.30 pm Monday to Friday, our answerphone will record your message and/or your order.

Information Service

If you need further information on any of our products, we recommend that you refer to our company's Client Information Service. We can give an immediate response to most queries. If necessary, we will check details with manufacturers and call you back within approximately 2 to 3 hours.

1

Your name   Exercise 6E   Centre No   1

SUPERNET

YOUR GATEWAY TO THE WORLD

For just £14.00 (+ VAT) per month plus an initial payment of only £25.00 (+ VAT), you can be instantly connected to the rest of the world! With over 30 million users world-wide, the Internet is growing at an unbelievable 12% per month. Realise the potential for your organisation!

We realise you may need help – the SUPERNET Centre will be your local advice point – always there when you need us.

Let us take all the worry out of your technological information and communications systems.

SETTING-UP PACKAGE (£25.00 + VAT at 17.5 % = £ 29.38)

Configuration of computer and modem
Fully-licensed software
Set-up of Internet account
Sign-up registration charge

Save 10 % if you pay for 1 year in advance - £22.00 saving!

The SUPERNET Centre is open for Setting-up from
9.00 am to 6.00 pm   Monday to Thursday
9.00 am to 8.00 pm   Friday to Saturday
10.00 am to 4.00 pm   Sunday

Just bring along your PC – we'll do the rest.
(Booking advised – Tel: Matthias Schneider or James Hall on 01234-1098765)

We realise you may not be able to leave the office – we'll come to you. FREE setting-up session within 8 mile radius. £15.00 fee for 9 to 15 miles radius

SYSTEM CHECK

Your IBM compatible PC will need:

Windows 3.1	4 Mb RAM	5 Mb free hard disk space
Windows 95	8 Mb RAM	20 Mb free hard disk space
Apple Macintosh	8 Mb RAM	5 Mb free hard disk space

Still teetering on the brink? Take the plunge. SUPERNET is your guarantee of a safe landing!

Supernet Centre

Your name   Exercise 6D   RSA Centre No

Terms

Pre-paid by 1 week or cash on delivery. Bank or trade references will take about 10 days; after this clearance time we will accept cheques. Returned or re-presented cheques will be charged at £15 on each occasion.

Your signature on delivery acknowledges receipt of all the goods shown on the invoice at the price given and in good condition. Claims can be accepted only on concerns regarding quality. Contact the Client Information Service in the unlikely event of such a problem. We will do our best to resolve the issue to your satisfaction.

We reserve the right not to accept orders, and all goods remain our property until they have been paid for.

Delivery

Refer to our map (on separate page at front of catalogue) to determine the day of the week when deliveries are made to your area. The minimum order amount is shown on this page. We feel sure you will appreciate that an order must be sufficiently large to justify **free delivery.**

Product Information

The following information is given in our catalogue and is displayed clearly in the warehouse for cash and carry clients:

Country of origin
Gluten-free products
Organically grown or produced products
Sugar-free products
Unit price
Unit size
Vegan products
Warehouse location codes

It is our intention to achieve our target of supplying all of our clients with all of the goods ordered on the date promised. You can help us to help you by preparing your order before telephoning.

2

NEW CARE CENTRES OPENED THIS YEAR

CENTRE NAME	SPECIAL FACILITIES	AVAILABLE PLACES	
		MALES	FEMALES
Centres in Lancashire			
Astonbury	All rooms en suite	8	10
Mountain View	Entertainment rota	15	15
The Redway	Health, fitness club	16	14
Centres in Yorkshire and Humberside			
Holly Grove	Games, activities	6	14
Lakeland House	Music room	12	8
Sunny Vale	Entertainment rota	10	10

Full details of the facilities at each Care Centre are available on request from Head Office. Cost of care varies between centres.

Your name Exercise 6E Centre No   2

Whether you are a small business user or you use a computer at home for study and general interest, we can offer you expert help. Our specialist technicians are well trained and they speak your language. We won't confuse you with unnecessary jargon – just tell us what you want from your computer and we'll tell you how to get started.

Many of our recent customers, who were new to computer use are now happily using E-mail to communicate with friends and colleagues for business or pleasure.

Students of all ages can enjoy access to an endless source of information in the form of text and graphics.

Business users can be sure that the information in their reports is up-to-date and relevant.

Anyone who has an interest or hobby can communicate with others of a like mind through a News group.

OPEN 7 DAYS – ALWAYS THERE WHEN YOU NEED US

WHY WAIT – JOIN THE INTERNET CROWD TODAY!

SUPERNET TEL 01234-1098765

Let us take all the worry out of your technological information and communications systems.

Supernet Centre

Log of technician call-outs by time period over the last year

UNIT CALL-OUTS	NUMBER OF RECORDED VISITS		AVERAGE VISIT TIME
	JANUARY TO JUNE	AUGUST TO DECEMBER	
Acting Technician: Barry Stevens			
Finance Unit	5	5	55 mins
Marketing Unit	3	7	1 hr 10 mins
Personnel Unit	7	4	35 mins
Acting Technician: Dianne Weston			
Clerical Unit	15	17	15 mins
Executive Unit	6	4	1 hr 15 mins
Export Unit	3	5	45 mins
Acting Technician: Herman Van Der Gouw			
Purchasing Unit	6	7	50 mins
Sales Unit	8	12	1 hr 20 mins
Stores Unit	2	4	30 mins

The log has identified a significant trend for increased technician visits during the second half of the year. The visit time spent in each unit shows a marked variance and further analysis will be conducted to ascertain the reasons behind this.

NEW PROPERTIES

PROPERTY AREAS	NUMBER OF ROOMS		GARAGE	PRICE
	TOTAL	BEDROOMS		
Semi-detached Properties				
MERSELEY	4	2	N	£48,000.00
WINDY VIEW	7	3	N	£65,000.00
ROOK LEA	8	3	Y	£82,000.00
Detached Properties				
KINGSWAY	8	3	Y	£94,000.00
ASTERBY	8	4	Y	£98,000.00
PENBOROUGH	11	5	Y	£125,000.00
Terraced Properties				
FIRTH BRIDGE	3	1	Y	£32,000.00
DEVERTON	6	2	N	£58,000.00
BARWALK	9	4	Y	£65,000.00

The above properties are new on the market this week and are therefore not displayed in our current brochure. Full written details are available from the office receptionist but photographs may still be awaited.

Unit 8
Exercise 8A

ACE BUSINESS SERVICES

246 Park View
LEEDS LS1 6RD

Tel no: 0113 246589   Fax no: 0113 246577

today's date

Mr Barry Fields
J D Fields & Co Ltd
Devenedge Road
BRADFORD
BD17 4RW

Dear Mr Fields

Thank you for your letter which we received last week. Unfortunately, the person to whom you addressed the letter left the company several months ago, which is the reason for the delay in our reply.

However, I have now passed your letter to our Customer Care Department for them to respond to the issues you raise. Part of the company's fundamental philosophy is to match all aspects of our business with customer satisfaction.

I note from your letter that you have a number of queries regarding our customised business services. One of our sales advisers would be pleased to visit you, at a mutually convenient time, in order to discuss your particular requirements more fully. This is a completely free service offered by our company. If you would like to take advantage of this offer, please contact our Sales Department on Extension 153.

If you require any additional information please do not hesitate to contact us again.

Yours sincerely

Melanie Parkes
ADMINISTRATION CLERK

Unit 9
Exercise 9A

ACE BUSINESS SERVICES

246 Park View
LEEDS LS1 6RD

Tel no: 0113 246589   Fax no: 0113 246577

today's date

Mr Barry Fields
J D Fields & Co Ltd
Devenedge Road
BRADFORD
BD17 4RW

Dear Mr Fields

Thank you for your letter which we received last week. Unfortunately, the person to whom you addressed the letter left the company several months ago, which is the reason for the delay in our reply.

However, I have now passed you letter to our Customer Care Department for them to respond to the issues you raise. Part of the company's fundamental philosophy is to match all aspects of our business with customer satisfaction.

In particular we offer:

a) Guaranteed delivery of any items ordered within 14 days from initial order.

b) No quibble exchange or refund for damaged or unwanted goods within 28 days of purchase.

c) On-going support and advice through our Telephone Hotline.

If you require any additional information please do not hesitate to contact us again.

Yours sincerely

Melanie Parkes
ADMINISTRATION CLERK

Copy: Customer Care Department
       File

Copy: Customer Care Department ✓
       File

Copy: Paula Denny
       File ✓

ACE BUSINESS SERVICES

246 Park View
LEEDS LS1 6RD

Tel no: 0113 246589   Fax no: 0113 246577

Our ref: VH/TS/564

today's date

Miss Tara Schmidt
14 New Ridgeway Road
BRISTOL BS4 2TR

Dear Miss Schmidt

Thank you for your recent enquiry regarding our range of business services. We pride ourselves on offering excellent value for money and reliable, quality services. All our services can be individually tailored to meet your specific needs.

Our company operates to IIP standards and has over 15 years' experience in developing world class business services. We have a number of Personal Consultants operating in your area who would be pleased to review any aspect of our business with you.

In relation to your enquiry about the purchase of computer equipment, we offer a specialist range of state-of-the-art computers designed to meet business needs. Please find enclosed our latest catalogue and price list.

All our systems come with a 12-month warranty for parts and labour, with the option to extend for a three or five year period.

I will ask our Personal Consultant Manager, Lee Johnson, to contact you as soon as possible in order to discuss your requirements further.

Yours sincerely

Vanessa Hartley
Business Development Manager

Encs

Copy: Lee Johnson
      File

Copy: Lee Johnson ✓
      File

Copy: Lee Johnson
      File✓

ACE BUSINESS SERVICES

MEMORANDUM

FROM: Harriet Janson, Personnel Assistant
TO: Kevin O'Flannagan, Purchasing Clerk
REF: GB/457
DATE: today's

STAFF DEVELOPMENT IN HEALTH AND SAFETY

We have received your application for staff development/training in the area of Health and Safety.

A copy of your application has been forwarded to your line manager, Paula Denny, for approval of your release from standard duties on one of the proposed training dates. Once this is confirmed we shall be able to reserve a definite place for you.

In accordance with our standard procedures you will be required to undertake the following prior to the event:

1) Read the Health and Safety procedures and information in the booklet attached.

2) Complete the attached questionnaire based on your existing knowledge. You will need to take this with you to the training session.

3) Identify current Health and Safety work practices in your department and prepare an outline of where you think these may need to be improved.

At the end of the training session, please complete and return the blue Staff Development Evaluation SD4. Guidance for completing the form is on the back of the SD4. It is essential that we receive feedback from all participants.

Thank you for your interest in this event.

Encs

Copy: Paula Denny
      File

Copy: Paula Denny ✓
      File

Copy: Paula Denny
      File✓

SOCIETY ON THE NET

OUR FUTURE ON THE WORLD WIDE WEB

We are entering a new era in which our economies and social fabrics will be shaped by the globe's public and private data networks.

It is said that the Internet is one of the most significant developments of our time.

The Net stretches around the globe like an electronic spider's web, interweaving communication links so that people from every extremity of the earth can connect in one massive computerised society.

The speed at which the Net is developing is faster than any technological change ever seen before. It demonstrates the reality of the theory of *'increasing returns'* - the more the Net grows, the more reason it has to grow further.

Analysts have theorised about the possible future implications of the Internet. People will expect to be connected to the Net wherever they are - on a plane, in a car, on a bicycle or in their living rooms.

Net Opinions

There are currently two main schools of extreme opinion about the wider impacts of the Internet on society. To the left there is the *'wired community'* which views the Net as uncontrollable and advocates that

---

SOCIETY ON THE NET

this giant global network joining ordinary people cannot be managed or restrained by any State or corporation.

To the right there are politicians, regulators and governments who seek to control the Web. Right-wingers can be torn between the desire to have a high-tech infrastructure for their economies and the fear that an uncontrollable universal network might prove extremely subversive.

Occupying the middle ground are those who understand the issues but believe that the 'worst-case' scenarios are unlikely. Optimism arises from the belief that today's hype about the Information Superhighway will be tomorrow's understatement. The access, mobility and ability to effect change are what will make the 21st century so different from the present.

Net Growth

It is envisaged that by the turn of the millennium there will be over half a billion users linked to the Net.

Net Futures

We are entering a new era in which our economies and social fabrics will be shaped by the globe's public and private data networks.

By its nature it is subversive and it will bring an end to many traditional notions of Western-style economics such as taxation, national currencies and national borders. National frontiers will continue to shrink as we

STAFF DEVELOPMENT EVENT - INTERNET TRAINING

DEPARTMENTAL ARRANGEMENTS

SESSIONAL
ARRANGEMENTS

EMPLOYEE NAME	EMPLOYEE POSITION	TRAINING SESSION DATE	TRAINING SESSION START TIME
Marketing and Sales Departments			
ALLAN, F	Sales Co-ordinator	7 October	10.30 am
COOKE, V	Marketing Officer	7 October	10.30 am
BROWN, L	Marketing Assistant	23 October	9.30 am
YOKOVIC, M	Sales Manager	23 October	9.30 am
JAMIESON, D	Marketing Director	24 October	10.00 am
Purchasing Department and Stores			
DENNY, P	Purchasing Manager	7 October	10.30 am
SHARMA, Y	Assistant Stores Manager	7 October	10.30 am
BRADY, A	Senior Purchasing Officer	23 October	9.30 am
MILTON, G	Stores Manager	23 October	9.30 am
BEDDOWS, J	Transport Manager	24 October	10.00 am
Personnel and Central Administration Departments			
JANSON, H	Personnel Assistant	7 October	10.30 am
O'MALLEY, B	Personnel Assistant	7 October	10.30 am
COOKE, R	Administration Co-ordinator	23 October	9.30 am
MACBETH, G	Personnel Manager	23 October	9.30 am
FOGGERY, N	Administration Manager	24 October	10.00 am

Internet Training Sessions for the staff named above will be held in Room C437. All staff are expected to attend on the dates and times stipulated.

SOCIETY ON THE NET

become inhabitants of the 'Virtual Society' or cyberspace. It also means an end to our concepts of intellectual property copyright.

National economic boundaries, already blurred by the use of private financial dealing networks, will cease to exist in a few years and companies will have to re-engineer the way they conduct their business. This massive change will emanate from three events. Firstly, the proliferation of personal computers in the office and home and their integration with the television and telephone. Secondly, the cost of international phone calls (and data communications in general) will reduce drastically. Thirdly, there will be an almost global desire by governments to deregulate and privatise the telecommunications industry.

Although it may be relatively easy to grasp the idea of connecting the globe's computers together over the telephone lines, it may be more difficult to fully realise just how much our lives will change as a result of such a simple concept.

3

ACE BUSINESS SERVICES

MEMORANDUM

FROM: Sam Byron, Computer Services Manager
TO: J Beddows, Transport Manager
REF: SB/JB/int56
DATE: today's

INTERNET TRAINING

We have received your application for staff development/training in the area of new technology. As part of the company's strategy to keep all staff up-to-date with information technology developments we are offering a number of training sessions on the Internet.

I am pleased to confirm that a place has been reserved for you. If you are unable to attend on the date and times shown below, please notify Personnel immediately so that we can re-allocate the place to another member of staff.

J Beddows, Transport Manager: 24 October at 10.00 am.

As part of our standard procedure, we require you to complete the green Staff Development Form SD3 along with the signature of your line manager. The form is in duplicate – please send the top copy to Personnel and retain one copy for yourself.

At the end of the training session, please complete and return the blue Staff Development Evaluation SD4. Guidance for completing the form is on the back of the SD4. It is essential that we receive feedback from all participants.

Other training events planned for this year are detailed below. I would be grateful if you could let me know which of these would be useful for you to attend.

a) Word 97 for Windows
b) Excel Spreadsheets
c) Video Conferencing
d) Access Database
e) E-mail (beginners and advanced)
f) PowerPoint
g) Microsoft Publisher

Copy: Personnel
       File

Copy: Personnel ✓
       File

Copy: Personnel
       File ✓

ACE BUSINESS SERVICES

MEMORANDUM

FROM: Sam Byron, Computer Services Manager
TO: G Milton, Stores Manager
REF: SB/JB/int56
DATE: today's

INTERNET TRAINING

We have received your application for staff development/training in the area of new technology. We are offering a number of training sessions on the Internet. I am pleased to confirm that a place has been reserved for you. If you are unable to attend on the date and times shown below, please notify Personnel immediately so that we can re-allocate the place to another member of staff.

G Milton, Stores Manager: 23 October at 9.30 am.

As part of our standard procedure, we require you to complete the green Staff Development Form SD3 along with the signature of your line manager. The form is in duplicate – please send the top copy to Personnel and retain one copy for yourself. At the end of the training session, please complete and return the blue Staff Development Evaluation SD4. Guidance for completing the form is on the back of the SD4. It is essential that we receive feedback from all participants.

Other planned training events are detailed below. Please let me know which of these you would like to attend.

a) Access Database
b) E-mail (beginners and advanced)
c) Excel Spreadsheets
d) Microsoft Publisher
e) PowerPoint
f) Video Conferencing
g) Word 97 for Windows

Copy: Personnel
       File

GROUP GUIDE

KIRKDALE PENNINE SPA

Welcome to the comprehensive group guide to Kirkdale Pennine Spa.

The Guide is designed to help you and your group to get as much enjoyment as possible from your day out in Kirkdale Pennine Spa.

You will find a complete list of local attractions including The Waterfront, Cedar Abbey and the City Art Gallery. Contact names, telephone numbers, admission prices and opening hours are given for each venue. Many of our attractions offer special rates for groups. Please call the named official to get some help in creating an interesting and informative visit.

The Tourist Information Office for Kirkdale Pennine Spa and district will be happy to help you to plan an interesting and successful day for your visit. Simply telephone Susan Bywater on 01484-646 5636 with details of your group numbers, ages, special interests etc. A customised itinerary will be drawn up and returned to you. Susan will even make all the arrangements for you if you wish. A fee of £10 - £20 is charged according to the complexity of the task.

Monday – Friday   9.30 am – 5.00 pm
Saturday and Sunday   10.00 am – 6.00 pm

The Services section of the group guide gives details of local tourist information centres, regional railways, airports, and bus and coach operators. A well-developed public transport system puts Kirkdale Pennine Spa firmly on the map. Our very successful Park and Ride scheme has been in operation for two years now, and is used by thousands of tourists annually.

1

GROUP GUIDE

The City Hopper and City Guide mini-buses offer cheap and frequent transport around the City. The City Guide buses have a local guide on board to point out places of interest along the way. The City Hopper fare is just 20p wherever you want to go. You can just hop on any of the distinctive yellow buses, hand over your 20 p fare, and hop off again at any bus stop. Many visitors really appreciate the journey by Hopper from the Waterfront to the Abbey – a walk of only half a mile but many, many steps!

Two special supplements are published annually for sports lovers and music fans. These are sent to you automatically when you request a copy of the group guide. Dalefoot Stadium hosts many important sporting events – national and international. The City Theatre and Royal Concert Hall are popular venues for performances covering the whole spectrum from opera to Oasis!

There's so much on offer in this famous Spa and the beautiful countryside of the surrounding area. Call us today to arrange your stay! The Guide is designed to help you and your group to get as much enjoyment as possible from your day out in Kirkdale Pennine Spa.

2

KIRKDALE PENNINE SPA

ACCOMMODATION LIST

Accommodation grades are based on accessibility, cleanliness, type of accommodation and customer service standards. The price range is based on one person staying for one night except for self-catering prices which are shown as per week for the property. Hotel prices include bed, breakfast and evening meal.

TYPE OF ACCOMMODATION	BEDROOMS	GRADE	ACCOMMODATION DETAILS	PRICE RANGE (£)
Hotels				
Ellam Lodge	4	A		60.00 – 85.00
The Elms	10	A		60.00 – 90.00
Old Bank Hall	3	B		35.00 – 50.00
Sugden Howe	7	B		50.00 – 70.00
Linden House	5	C		30.00 – 49.00
Bed and Breakfast				
Beck Cottage	3	A		25.00 – 39.00
Chapel End Farm	2	B		18.00 – 25.00
Whin Fell House	3	B		20.00 – 30.00
Low Stone Farm	2	B		20.00 – 35.00
Waterside Mill	4	B		19.00 – 29.00
Self-Catering				
The Grain Loft	1	A		200.00 – 350.00
Hill End	3	A		250.00 – 350.00
Peat Moor Barn	4	B		300.00 – 500.00
Byrne Farm	2	C		90.00 – 200.00
Chapel End Cottage	2	C		110.00 – 210.00

KIRKDALE PENNINE SPA

The Guide is designed to help you to get as much enjoyment as possible from your day out in Kirkdale Pennine Spa.

You will find a complete list of local attractions including The Waterfront, Cedar Abbey and the City Art Gallery. Contact names, telephone numbers, admission prices and opening hours are given for each venue.

The Tourist Information Office for Kirkdale Pennine Spa and district will be happy to help you to plan an interesting and successful day. Simply telephone Susan Bywater on 01484-646 5636 with details of your special interests etc.

Consider the following alternatives:

Cedar Abbey
City Art Gallery
Kirkdale Crafts
Maggie's Mill Shop
Rowan Falls
Streamside Walk
The Waterfront

The Tourist Information Office is open as follows:

Monday – Friday	9.30 am – 5.00 pm
Saturday and Sunday	10.00 am – 6.00 pm

Winter activities include tea dances in the Victoria Ballroom for the young at heart and the latest in winter sports technology at the Fellside Ski Slope for the young in body!

There is a wide variety of accommodation in the area from first class hotels to modest self-catering establishments. Ask for details before you plan your outing – you may decide to stay over for 3 or 4 days!

Title	FirstName	LastName	Address1	Address2	City	PostalCode	Membership
Ms	Judith	Appleyard	Flat 12	Archer House	LEEDS	LS2 6FD	Gym
Miss	Lana	Ephraim	293 Thorncliffe Way	Farringdon	BRADFORD	BD5 0MX	Beauty
Mrs	Amelia	Staines	34 Durham Avenue	Whitfield	LEEDS	LS23 8HT	Full
Miss	Gillian	Winterburn	Winter Cottage	Well Bank	BRADFORD	BD17 9NB	Full

---

MEMORANDUM

To: Susan Bywater, Tourist Information Office, Kirkdale Pennine Spa

From: Kenneth Martin, Tourism Officer

Date: Date of typing

I hope that you found the recent training day to be stimulating and relevant. As promised, I am writing to give further details of workshops which are scheduled to take place in the Autumn.

In your part of the district, it is our intention to focus marketing research on group activities and facilities with a view to encouraging and expanding our provision. The new outdoor education division at Dalefoot College will be working with us on this venture.

Students following programmes in leisure, tourism, business studies and outdoor recreation will assist in the research aspects under the direction of the College staff. We have agreed an action plan with those concerned.

Within the next few days, you should hear from Lyn Richard, Co-ordinator of Leisure and Recreation Programmes at the Dalefoot College. I hope that you and she can work together to oversee the students' research work. I enclose a copy of the action plan.

Each group of students is to prepare and submit a report and presentation to the first workshop in September. Monthly meetings will be held to determine marketing strategies and identify resource needs so that promotional materials are ready for publication soon after Christmas.

I think that you and your staff will enjoy working with the students. Obviously, they will need considerable guidance in the early stages and they will be supported by their College tutors. I have already spoken to the students allocated to your area. Many of them are local residents keen to help in developing facilities and opportunities on home ground.

I wish you and your teams every success.

Copy: Lyn Richard
        File

Enc

Our Ref: GB/NS

Date of typing

Miss Lana Ephraim
293 Thorncliffe Way
Farringdon
BRADFORD
BD5 0MX

Dear Lana

Welcome to ACE Bodies, the in-house health and fitness club of ACE Business Services.

I have pleasure in enclosing your membership card and receipt for the membership fee. Hours of opening are shown on the card.

We look forward to seeing you soon for your introductory sessions where you will be given expert help in designing a practical and enjoyable exercise programme.

Yours sincerely

Gina Biondo
MANAGER

Encs

Our Ref: GB/NS

Date of typing

«Title» «FirstName» «LastName»
«Address1»
«Address2»
«City»
«PostalCode»

Dear «FirstName»

Welcome to ACE Bodies, the in-house health and fitness club of ACE Business Services.

I have pleasure in enclosing your membership card and receipt for the membership fee. Hours of opening are shown on the card.

We look forward to seeing you soon for your introductory sessions where you will be given expert help in designing a practical and enjoyable exercise programme.

Yours sincerely

Gina Biondo
MANAGER

Encs

Unit 12
Exercise 12C – Merged documents

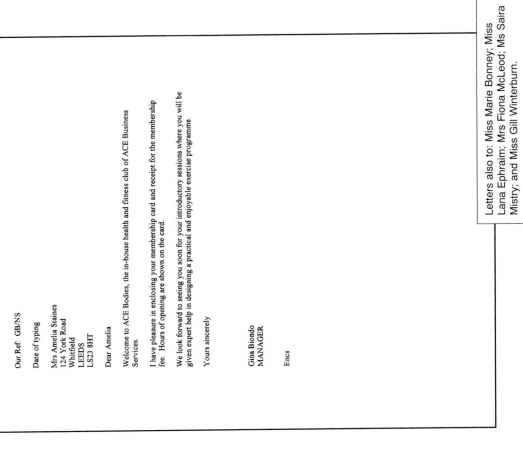

Our Ref: GB/NS

Date of typing

Mrs Amelia Staines
124 York Road
Whitfield
LEEDS
LS23 8HT

Dear Amelia

Welcome to ACE Bodies, the in-house health and fitness club of ACE Business Services.

I have pleasure in enclosing your membership card and receipt for the membership fee. Hours of opening are shown on the card.

We look forward to seeing you soon for your introductory sessions where you will be given expert help in designing a practical and enjoyable exercise programme.

Yours sincerely

Gina Biondo
MANAGER

Encs

Letters also to: Miss Marie Bonney; Miss Lana Ephraim; Mrs Fiona McLeod; Ms Saira Mistry; and Miss Gill Winterburn.

Unit 12
Exercise 12B – Data source

Title	FirstName	LastName	Address1	Address2	City	PostalCode	Membership
Miss	Lana	Ephraim	293 Thorncliffe Way	Farringdon	BRADFORD	BD5 0MX	Beauty
Mrs	Amelia	Staines	124 York Road	Whitfield	LEEDS	LS23 8HT	Full
Miss	Gill	Winterburn	Winter Cottage	Well Bank	BRADFORD	BD17 9NB	Full
Ms	Saira	Mistry	3 The Crescent	Eastfield	LEEDS	LS10 3JW	Gym
Mrs	Fiona	McLeod	The Coach House	Hallenshaw	BRADFORD	BD16 7HH	Beauty
Miss	Marie	Bonney	7 Severn Street	Whitfield	LEEDS	LS23 6DD	Gym

Unit 13
Exercise 13A – UNIT13DATA1

Title	FirstName	LastName	Address1	Address2	City	PostalCode	Membership	Sub due date
Miss	Lana	Ephraim	293 Thorncliffe Way	Farringdon	BRADFORD	BD5 0MX	Beauty	31/12/98
Mrs	Amelia	Staines	124 York Road	Whitfield	LEEDS	LS23 8HT	Beauty	31/12/98
Mrs	Gill	Brooke	Grafton House	Well Bank	BRADFORD	BD17 9BH	Full	31/7/98
Ms	Saira	Mistry	3 The Crescent	Eastfield	LEEDS	LS10 3JW	Gym	30/6/98
Mrs	Fiona	McLeod	The Coach House	Hallenshaw	BRADFORD	BD16 7HH	Full	31/12/98
Miss	Marie	Bonney	7 Severn Street	Whitfield	LEEDS	LS23 6DD	Gym	30/4/98

Unit 13
Exercise 13B – Sorted by LastName

Title	FirstName	LastName	Address1	Address2	City	PostalCode	Membership	Sub due date
Miss	Marie	Bonney	7 Severn Street	Whitfield	LEEDS	LS23 6DD	Gym	30/4/98
Mrs	Gill	Brooke	Grafton House	Well Bank	BRADFORD	BD17 9BH	Full	31/7/98
Miss	Lana	Ephraim	293 Thorncliffe Way	Farringdon	BRADFORD	BD5 0MX	Beauty	31/12/98
Mrs	Fiona	McLeod	The Coach House	Hallenshaw	BRADFORD	BD16 7HH	Full	31/12/98
Ms	Saira	Mistry	3 The Crescent	Eastfield	LEEDS	LS10 3JW	Gym	30/6/98
Mrs	Amelia	Staines	124 York Road	Whitfield	LEEDS	LS23 8HT	Beauty	31/12/98

Exercise 13B – Sorted by SubDueDate

Title	FirstName	LastName	Address1	Address2	City	PostalCode	Membership	Sub due date
Miss	Lana	Ephraim	293 Thorncliffe Way	Farringdon	BRADFORD	BD5 0MX	Beauty	31/12/98
Mrs	Fiona	McLeod	The Coach House	Hallenshaw	BRADFORD	BD16 7HH	Full	31/12/98
Mrs	Amelia	Staines	124 York Road	Whitfield	LEEDS	LS23 8HT	Beauty	31/12/98
Mrs	Gill	Brooke	Grafton House	Well Bank	BRADFORD	BD17 9BH	Full	31/7/98
Ms	Saira	Mistry	3 The Crescent	Eastfield	LEEDS	LS10 3JW	Gym	30/6/98
Miss	Marie	Bonney	7 Severn Street	Whitfield	LEEDS	LS23 6DD	Gym	30/4/98

Exercise 13C – Main document

ACE BUSINESS SERVICES

246 Park View
LEEDS LS1 6RD

Tel no: 0113 246589   Fax no: 0113 246577

Our Ref: GB/DB

Date of typing

«Title» «FirstName» «LastName»
«Address1»
«Address2»
«City»
«PostalCode»

Dear «FirstName»

'ACE BODIES' – MEMBERSHIP DETAILS

As I am sure you already know, our in-house health and fitness club has been a tremendous success. Since starting up 6 months ago with approximately 25 brave and energetic employees, our membership has grown to over 150! The most popular activities are still multi-gym and exercise classes of various types but the beauty therapy section is expanding quickly and extra evening sessions are to begin next month.

We have recently computerised our membership records (with considerable help from Louise Allersby in Computer Operations). This letter has been produced to allow us to check your details. Your membership type and subscription due date are shown below:

Membership: «Membership»   Subscription due date:«Sub_due_date»

Please inform us if this information is not correct so that we can amend it. We would also like to hear from you if your name and address details are incorrect in any way. If we do not hear from you, we will assume we got it right!

Thank you for your co-operation and wishing you the best of health.

Yours sincerely

Gina Biondo
MANAGER

ACE BUSINESS SERVICES

246 Park View
LEEDS LS1 6RD

Tel no: 0113 246589   Fax no: 0113 246577

Our Ref: GB/DB

Date of typing

Mrs Fiona McLeod
The Coach House
Hallenshaw
BRADFORD
BD16 7HH

Dear Fiona

'ACE BODIES' – MEMBERSHIP DETAILS

As I am sure you already know, our in-house health and fitness club has been a tremendous success. Since starting up 6 months ago with approximately 25 brave and energetic employees, our membership has grown to over 150! The most popular activities are still multi-gym and exercise classes of various types but the beauty therapy section is expanding quickly and extra evening sessions are to begin next month.

We have recently computerised our membership records (with considerable help from Louise Allersby in Computer Operations). This letter has been produced to allow us to check your details. Your membership type and subscription due date are shown below:

Membership: Full   Subscription due date: 31/12/98

Please inform us if this information is not correct so that we can amend it. We would also like to hear from you if your name and address details are incorrect in any way. If we do not hear from you, we will assume we got it right!

Thank you for your co-operation and wishing you the best of health.

Yours sincerely

Gina Biondo
MANAGER

Letter also to: Mrs Gill Brooke.

ACE BUSINESS SERVICES

246 Park View
LEEDS LS1 6RD

Tel no: 0113 246589   Fax no: 0113 246577

Our Ref: GB/DB

Date of typing

Mrs Amelia Staines
124 York Road
Whitfield
LEEDS
LS23 8HT

Dear Amelia

'ACE BODIES' – MEMBERSHIP DETAILS

As I am sure you already know, our in-house health and fitness club has been a tremendous success. Since starting up 6 months ago with approximately 25 brave and energetic employees, our membership has grown to over 150! The most popular activities are still multi-gym and exercise classes of various types but the beauty therapy section is expanding quickly and extra evening sessions are to begin next month.

We have recently computerised our membership records (with considerable help from Louise Allersby in Computer Operations). This letter has been produced to allow us to check your details. Your membership type and subscription due date are shown below:

Membership: Beauty   Subscription due date: 31/12/98

Please inform us if this information is not correct so that we can amend it. We would also like to hear from you if your name and address details are incorrect in any way. If we do not hear from you, we will assume we got it right!

Thank you for your co-operation and wishing you the best of health.

Yours sincerely

Gina Biondo
MANAGER

Letters also to: Miss Marie Bonney; Ms Saira Mistry.

ACE BUSINESS SERVICES

246 Park View
LEEDS LS1 6RD

Tel no: 0113 246589   Fax no: 0113 246577

Our Ref: GB/DB

Date of typing

Ms Saira Mistry
3 The Crescent
Eastfield
LEEDS
LS10 3JW

Dear Saira

'ACE BODIES' – MEMBERSHIP DETAILS

As I am sure you already know, our in-house health and fitness club has been a tremendous success. Since starting up 6 months ago with approximately 25 brave and energetic employees, our membership has grown to over 150! The most popular activities are still multi-gym and exercise classes of various types but the beauty therapy section is expanding quickly and extra evening sessions are to begin next month.

We have recently computerised our membership records (with considerable help from Louise Allersby in Computer Operations). This letter has been produced to allow us to check your details. Your membership type and subscription due date are shown below:

Membership: Gym   Subscription due date: 30/6/98

Please inform us if this information is not correct so that we can amend it. We would also like to hear from you if your name and address details are incorrect in any way. If we do not hear from you, we will assume we got it right!

Thank you for your co-operation and wishing you the best of health.

Yours sincerely

Gina Biondo
MANAGER

Letter also to: Miss Marie Bonney

ACE BUSINESS SERVICES

246 Park View
LEEDS LS1 6RD

Tel no: 0113 246589   Fax no: 0113 246577

Our Ref: GB/DB

Date of typing

Miss Lana Ephraim
293 Thorncliffe Way
Farringdon
BRADFORD
BD5 0MX

Dear Lana

'ACE BODIES' – MEMBERSHIP DETAILS

As I am sure you already know, our in-house health and fitness club has been a tremendous success. Since starting up 6 months ago with approximately 25 brave and energetic employees, our membership has grown to over 150! The most popular activities are still multi-gym and exercise classes of various types but the beauty therapy section is expanding quickly and extra evening sessions are to begin next month.

We have recently computerised our membership records (with considerable help from Louise Allersby in Computer Operations). This letter has been produced to allow us to check your details. Your membership type and subscription due date are shown below:

Membership: Beauty   Subscription due date: 31/12/98

Please inform us if this information is not correct so that we can amend it. We would also like to hear from you if your name and address details are incorrect in any way. If we do not hear from you, we will assume we got it right!

Thank you for your co-operation and wishing you the best of health.

Yours sincerely

Gina Biondo
MANAGER

Letter also to: Mrs Amelia Staines.

Unit 14
Exercise 14A

FirstName	LastName	Address 1	Address 2	City	PostalCode	Dept
Roche	Sandra	37 Denfield Avenue	Farringdon	BRADFORD	BD5 5NQ	Sales
Roper	James	Hill Crest	Hallenshaw	BRADFORD	BD16 3RF	Accounts
Loboda	Francis	17 Moorend Grove	Whitfield	LEEDS	LS23 5SL	Production
Hartley	Shirley	160 Sandhall Road	Well Bank	BRADFORD	BD17 2RA	Sales
Blagbrough	Alan	13 New Street	Eastfield	LEEDS	LS10 9SD	Marketing
Akhtar	Saima	26 Shaw Road	Whitfield	LEEDS	LS23 8EL	Purchasing
Broadbent	Roger	Hebble View	Hallenshaw	BRADFORD	BD16 8JT	Sales
Charnock	Alicia	10 Westgate	Well Bank	BRADFORD	BD17 3LW	Sales
Dale	Colin	1 Cromwell Drive	Farringdon	BRADFORD	BD5 4NS	Accounts
Fitzgerald	Sonia	16 Arncliffe Lane	Dalefoot	BRADFORD	BD21 2LD	Marketing

Unit 13
Exercise 13G – UNIT13DATA

FirstName	LastName	Address 1	Address 2	City	PostalCode	Sub due date
Lana	Ephraim	293 Thorncliffe Way	Farringdon	BRADFORD	BD5 0MX	31/12/98
Fiona	McLeod	The Coach House	Hallenshaw	BRADFORD	BD16 7HH	31/12/98
Amelia	Staines	124 York Road	Whitfield	LEEDS	LS23 8HT	31/12/98
Gill	Brooke	Grafton House	Well Bank	BRADFORD	BD17 9BH	31/7/98
Saira	Mistry	3 The Crescent	Eastfield	LEEDS	LS10 3JW	30/6/98
Marie	Bonney	7 Severn Street	Whitfield	LEEDS	LS23 6DD	30/4/98

ACE BUSINESS SERVICES

MEMORANDUM

To: Sandra Roche, Sales Department

From: Simon Queensbury, Personnel Administrator

Date: Date of typing

Staff Induction

Welcome to ACE! I hope that your first few days with us have been interesting and enjoyable, and that you are beginning to settle in to the department and the Company.

In addition to the Health and Safety and Departmental Induction sessions, we are planning an induction morning to give more details of our expansion plans and to allow you to see more of other departments and personnel.

Please come along to the Board Room at 10.00 am on Tuesday 10 May. Coffee and biscuits will be served and the meeting should be finished at approximately 12 noon.

I enclose some literature for you to read prior to the meeting and look forward to seeing you on the date given above.

Enc

Memos also to: Roger Broadbent; Alicia Charnock; and Shirley Hartley.

ACE BUSINESS SERVICES

MEMORANDUM

To: «FirstName» «LastName», «Dept» Department

From: Simon Queensbury, Personnel Administrator

Date: Date of typing

Staff Induction

Welcome to ACE! I hope that your first few days with us have been interesting and enjoyable, and that you are beginning to settle in to the department and the Company.

In addition to the Health and Safety and Departmental Induction sessions, we are planning an induction morning to give more details of our expansion plans and to allow you to see more of other departments and personnel.

Please come along to the Board Room at 10.00 am on Tuesday 10 May. Coffee and biscuits will be served and the meeting should be finished at approximately 12 noon.

I enclose some literature for you to read prior to the meeting and look forward to seeing you on the date given above.

Enc

LastName	FirstName	Address 1	Address 2	City	PostalCode	Dept	Grade	Appraisal	Payroll
Khan	Sofina	13 Whalley Road	Eastfield	LEEDS	LS10 4WA	Production	D	July	00682
Lawrence	Sarah	Highcroft	Burn Wood	BRADFORD	BD19 3AL	Purchasing	D	April	00449
Lewis	Katy	Howard Hall	Dalefoot	BRADFORD	BD21 5RT	Production	B	Sept	00236
Loboda	Francis	17 Moorend Grove	Whitfield	LEEDS	LS23 5SL	Production	D	Aug	01023
Morris	Graham	60 Sherby Drive	Dalefoot	BRADFORD	BD21 5LV	Production	A	Mar	00144
Petrovic	Tadeusz	Green House	Hallenshaw	BRADFORD	BD16 2EN	Purchasing	C	April	00132
Reed	Adam	8 Grange Road	Stonemount	BRADFORD	BD10 1NS	Sales	C	Feb	00672
Roche	Sandra	37 Denfield Grove	Farringdon	BRADFORD	BD5 5NQ	Sales	B	Aug	01021
Roper	Jim	Hill Crest	Hallenshaw	BRADFORD	BD16 3RF	Accounts	D	July	01022
Sawyer	Kevin	17 Badger Lane	Hollins	LEEDS	LS3 6HB	Marketing	B	Jan	00642
Shuvla	Milo	14 Cook Street	Eastfield	LEEDS	LS10 4EA	Production	D	July	00239
Southgate	Daniel	11 George Street	Whitfield	LEEDS	LS23 1TV	Production	D	July	00592

LastName	FirstName	Address 1	Address 2	City	PostalCode	Dept	Grade	Appraisal	Payroll
Akhtar	Saima	26 Shaw Road	Whitfield	LEEDS	LS23 8EL	Purchasing	D	July	01026
Broadbent	Roger	Hebble View	Hallenshaw	BRADFORD	BD16 8JT	Sales	A	July	01027
Calvert	Margaret	10 Ramsden Row	Dalefoot	BRADFORD	BD21 4SE	Accounts	C	May	00182
Charnock	Alicia	10 Westgate	Well Bank	BRADFORD	BD17 3LW	Sales	D	Aug	01028
Clare	Alison	Dale Head	Burn Wood	BRADFORD	BD19 7DH	Personnel	A	Aug	00201
Dale	Colin	1 Cromwell Drive	Farringdon	BRADFORD	BD5 4NS	Accounts	E	July	01029
Fielden	Jonathan	5 South Parade	Whitfield	LEEDS	LS23 7NP	Accounts	D	July	00437
Fitzgerald	Sonya	16 Arncliffe Lane	Dalefoot	BRADFORD	BD21 2LD	Marketing	B	Aug	01210
Gannon	Kathleen	8 Lea Grove	Well Bank	BRADFORD	BD17 7JS	Sales	E	Mar	00876
Hartley	Shirley	16 Sandhall Road	Well Bank	BRADFORD	BD17 2RA	Sales	D	July	01024
James	Iain	131 Lodge Grove	Stonemount	BRADFORD	BD10 9RA	Marketing	E	June	00997
Khalid	Mukhtar	13 South Parade	Whitfield	LEEDS	LS23 7PR	Sales	B	Oct	00434

LastName	FirstName	Address 1	Address 2	City	PostalCode	Dept	Grade	Appraisal	Payroll
Sykes	William	2 Oliver's Way	Arden	LEEDS	LS6 8RD	Production	B	Dec	00690
Sykes	Valerie	2 Oliver's Way	Arden	LEEDS	LS6 8RD	Sales	D	July	00591
Woodhead	Steven	4 Woodview Avenue	Well Bank	BRADFORD	BD17 7LA	Production	C	Jan	00668
Woodhead	Lee	52 Wakefield Road	Farringdon	BRADFORD	BD5 2DB	Production	D	July	00789
Zimmer	Marc	4 Woodhouse Road	Burn Wood	BRADFORD	BD19 9SH	Production	E	Dec	00671

ACE BUSINESS SERVICES

246 Park View
LEEDS LS1 6RD

Tel no: 0113 246589   Fax no: 0113 246577

Ref: SQ/«Payroll»

Date of typing

«FirstName» «LastName»
«Address1»
«Address2»
«City»
«PostalCode»

Dear «FirstName»

Annual Appraisal

I am writing to remind you that your annual appraisal discussion is to take place in «Appraisal». Grade «Grade» members of staff are to be appraised for the first time this year following consultation and information sessions.

Unless otherwise agreed, your immediate line manager will be your appraiser and preliminary meetings will take place approximately 4 weeks beforehand.

A full pack of documentation was issued during the earlier information session. If you require further copies, please contact me on Extension 242.

Yours sincerely

Simon Queensbury
Personnel Administrator

Unit 15
Document 1 – UNIT15DATA1

LastName	FirstName	Address 1	Address 2	City	PostalCode	Dept	Grade	Appraisal	Payroll	Car Reg
Broadbent	Roger	Hebble View	Hallenshaw	BRADFORD	BD16 8JT	Sales	A	July	01027	P 67 DAP
Clare	Alison	Dale Head	Burn Wood	BRADFORD	BD19 7DH	Personnel	A	Aug	00201	R104 ALI
Morris	Graham	60 Sherby Drive	Dalefoot	BRADFORD	BD21 5LV	Production	A	Mar	00144	P447 DUC
Philpott	Michael	Spring House	Hallenshaw	BRADFORD	BD16 2RL	Marketing	A	Aug	01036	P970 MPT
Anwar	Salome	10 Cliffe Avenue	Arden	LEEDS	LS6 6TP	Personnel	B	Aug	01038	N383 MSM
Calvert	Margaret	10 Ramsden Row	Dalefoot	BRADFORD	BD21 4SE	Accounts	B	May	00182	R416 PAM
Fitzgerald	Sonya	1 Field Side	Dalefoot	BRADFORD	BD21 2LD	Marketing	B	Aug	01210	P774 DBL
Khalid	Mukhtar	13 South Parade	Whitfield	LEEDS	LS23 7PR	Sales	B	Aug	00434	N494 PRM
Lewis	Katie	Howard Hall	Dalefoot	BRADFORD	BD21 5RT	Production	B	Sept	00236	R632 KTL
Moorby	Derek	Hazel Garth	Arden	LEEDS	LS6 8RD	Production	B	Aug	01041	P68 RED
Roche	Sandra	37 Denfield Lane	Farringdon	BRADFORD	BD5 5NQ	Sales	B	Aug	01021	N204 AND
Rowan	Paul	721 Leeds Road	Farringdon	BRADFORD	BD5 6NG	Production	B	Sept	01033	R333 WAN

Unit 14
Exercise 14D – Merged document

ACE BUSINESS SERVICES

246 Park View
LEEDS LS1 6RD

Tel no: 0113 246589   Fax no: 0113 246577

Ref: SQ/01026

Date of typing

Saima Akhtar
26 Shaw Road
Whitfield
LEEDS
LS23 8EL

Dear Saima

Annual Appraisal

I am writing to remind you that your annual appraisal discussion is to take place in July. Grade D members of staff are to be appraised for the first time this year following consultation and information sessions.

Unless otherwise agreed, your immediate line manager will be your appraiser and preliminary meetings will take place approximately 4 weeks beforehand.

A full pack of documentation was issued during the earlier information session. If you require further copies, please contact me on Extension 242.

Yours sincerely

Simon Queensbury
Personnel Administrator

Letters also to: Jonathan Fielden; Shirley Hartley; Sofina Khan; Jim Roper; Milo Shuvla; Daniel Southgate; Valerie Sykes; and Lee Woodhead.

LastName	FirstName	Address 1	Address 2	City	PostalCode	Dept	Grade	Appraisal	Payroll	Car Reg
Charnock	Alicia	10 Westgate	Well Bank	BRADFORD	BD17 3LW	Sales	D	Aug	01028	N703 GUA
Fielden	Jonathan	5 South Parade	Whitfield	LEEDS	LS23 7NP	Accounts	D	July	00437	
Hartley	Shirley	16 Sandhall Road	Well Bank	BRADFORD	BD17 2RA	Sales	D	July	01024	K173 WEL
Khan	Sofina	13 Whalley Road	Eastfield	LEEDS	LS10 4WA	Production	D	July	00682	
Lawrence	Sarah	Highcroft	Burn Wood	BRADFORD	BD19 3AL	Purchasing	D	April	00449	L490 REN
Roper	Jim	Hill Crest	Hallenshaw	BRADFORD	BD16 3RF	Accounts	D	July	01022	M721 PER
Shuvla	Milos	14 Cook Street	Eastfield	LEEDS	LS10 4EA	Production	D	July	00239	
Simha	Sohan	70 Cliffe View	Arden	LEEDS	LS6 6TF	Sales	D	Sept	01034	
Southgate	Daniel	11 George Street	Whitfield	LEEDS	LS23 1TV	Production	D	July	00592	
Woodhead	Lee	52 Wakefield Road	Farringdon	BRADFORD	BD5 2DB	Production	D	July	00789	
Zaleski	Mario	5 Moor Grove	Eastfield	LEEDS	LS10 5OM	Production	D	Sept	01040	
Zimmer	Marc	4 Woodhouse Road	Burn Wood	BRADFORD	BD19 9SH	Production	D	Dec	00671	
Dale	Colin	1 Cromwell Drive	Farringdon	BRADFORD	BD5 4NS	Purchasing	E	July	01029	M42 DCA

LastName	FirstName	Address 1	Address 2	City	PostalCode	Dept	Grade	Appraisal	Payroll	Car Reg
Sawyer	Kevin	17 Badger Lane	Hollins	LEEDS	LS3 6HB	Marketing	B	Jan	00642	M462 KEL
Sykes	William	2 Oliver's Way	Arden	LEEDS	LS6 8RD	Production	B	Dec	00690	P58 ROD
Woolf	Anya	7 Crag End	Dalefoot	BRADFORD	BD21 6XW	Sales	B	Aug	01039	N214 ASA
Akhtar	Saima	26 Shaw Road	Whitfield	LEEDS	LS23 8EL	Sales	C	July	01026	L446 BOL
Hussain	Leyla	34 Lister Drive	Burn Wood	BRADFORD	BD19 9HJ	Purchasing	C	Sept	01035	N196 UJX
Maud	Rita	6 Broadway	Stonemount	BRADFORD	BD10 6AW	Production	C	Aug	01042	L884 TAL
Petrovic	Tadeusz	Green House	Hallenshaw	BRADFORD	BD16 2EN	Purchasing	C	April	00132	P703 TED
Reed	Adam	8 Grange Road	Stonemount	BRADFORD	BD10 1NS	Sales	C	Feb	00672	L101 ADR
Stewart	Vikki	6 Vale Road	Hollins	LEEDS	LS10 4ES	Sales	C	Aug	01030	P996 LEM
Weir	Sharon	18 Duke's Square	Whitfield	LEEDS	LS23 7NO	Accounts	C	Sept	01037	J665 WXY
Woodhead	Steven	4 Woodview Avenue	Well Bank	BRADFORD	BD17 7LA	Production	C	Jan	00668	M175 SWK
Byrne	Sean	55 Anne's Way	Arden	LEEDS	LS6 5AA	Accounts	D	Aug	01044	
Challoner	Amy	3 Bailey Grove	Dalefoot	BRADFORD	BD21 5RT	Marketing	D	Aug	01031	K311 LEA

LastName	FirstName	Address 1	Address 2	City	PostalCode	Dept	Grade	Appraisal	Payroll	Car Reg
Gannon	Kathleen	8 Lea Grove	Well Bank	BRADFORD	BD17 7JS	Sales	E	Mar	00876	
James	Iain	131 Lodge Grove	Stonemount	BRADFORD	BD10 9RA	Marketing	E	June	00997	K714 NUJ
Riva	Rachel	20 Bank Street	Roundhill	BRADFORD	BD7 5LS	Production	E	Sept	01032	
Duncan	Matthew	10 Chapel Road	Farringdon	BRADFORD	BD5 8PA	Sales	E	Aug	01043	J611 RND

Title	Initials	Surname	Street	Town	Postcode	Pet
Mrs	H A	Bulmer	16 Southmead Lane	NORCHESTER	NR16 4SE	Cat
Mr	L	Halls	Rose Cottage	GLENDALE	GE10 3SG	Dog
Ms	M E	Kallo	10 Surrey Street	NORCHESTER	NR4 3RS	Dog
Mrs	B	Fyffe	3 Leyland Grove	GLENDALE	GE3 7DN	Dog
Mr	L G	Mann	62 Borough Road West	NORCHESTER	NR1 1HR	Dog
Ms	R S	West	Arran View	HARRISTON	HN3 8TN	Cat
Mrs	J	Harr	11 Sandy Road	GLENDALE	GE9 9SJ	Cat
Mrs	A M	Smith	33 Queens Road	NORCHESTER	NR8 3MA	Dog
Ms	J	Christie	136 Union Street	NORCHESTER	NR2 WNL	Dog
Mr	F R	Ciccone	11 Higher Falls	HARRISTON	HN6 4RF	Cat

ACE BUSINESS SERVICES

MEMORANDUM

To: «FirstName» «LastName», «Dept» Department

From: Tessa McLoughlin, Operations Manager

Ref: TM/OM/«Payroll»

Date: Date of typing

STAFF CAR PARKING

Redevelopment work on the Company's car parking facilities is almost completed. The new car park to the east of the site will be opened at the end of this month.

Staff travelling from Leeds are recommended to use the A580 and then Parkwood Road for ease of access (see attached map).

Passes will be issued over the next two weeks. Our records show the following car as registered in your name:

Vehicle Registration No: «Car_Reg»

Please inform me if you have changed your vehicle or if you would like to register a second vehicle.

Enc

ACE BUSINESS SERVICES

246 Park View
LEEDS LS1 6RD

Tel no: 0113 246589   Fax no: 0113 246577

Ref: JR/PetIns/NORCHESTER

Date of typing

«Title» «Initials» «Surname»
«Street»
«Town»
«Postcode»

Dear «Title» «Surname»

LOOKING AFTER YOUR BEST FRIEND

Thank you for your recent enquiry regarding insurance for family pets. As a caring pet owner, you want to make sure that your «Pet» gets the best treatment in case of injury or illness. Unfortunately, approximately one third of pets require veterinary treatment each year, and the fees can be a worry.

ACE Pet Insurance can give you peace of mind at a low cost. Cover can be individually tailored to suit your pet and can be extended to include holiday cancellation, theft, straying and death. Full details are enclosed.

For a free quotation and immediate cover, please ring our Hotline on 0115 254 3383. Alternatively, come along to meet our specially qualified staff at the Norchester Veterinary Centre on Wednesday 24 August between 6 pm and 9 pm. You will find that you can put your mind at rest for a small charge.

Yours sincerely

J Russell
Pet Insurance Manager

Enc

ACE BUSINESS SERVICES
MEMORANDUM

To: Graham Morris, Production Department

From: Tessa McLoughlin, Operations Manager

Ref: TM/OM/00144

Date: Date of typing

STAFF CAR PARKING

Redevelopment work on the Company's car parking facilities is almost completed. The new car park to the east of the site will be opened at the end of this month.

Staff travelling from Leeds are recommended to use the A580 and then Parkwood Road for ease of access (see attached map).

Passes will be issued over the next two weeks. Our records show the following car as registered in your name:

Vehicle Registration No: P447 DUC

Please inform me if you have changed your vehicle or if you would like to register a second vehicle.

Enc

Memos also to: Margaret Calvert; Amy Challoner; Sonya Fitzgerald; Katie Lewis; and Anya Woolf.

ACE BUSINESS SERVICES
246 Park View
LEEDS LS1 6RD

Tel no: 0113 246589   Fax no: 0113 246577

Ref: JR/PetIns/NORCHESTER

Date of typing

Ms M E Kallo
10 Surrey Street
NORCHESTER
NR4 3RS

Dear Ms Kallo

LOOKING AFTER YOUR BEST FRIEND

Thank you for your recent enquiry regarding insurance for family pets. As a caring pet owner, you want to make sure that your «Pet» gets the best treatment in case of injury or illness. Unfortunately, approximately one third of pets require veterinary treatment each year, and the fees can be a worry.

ACE Pet Insurance can give you peace of mind at a low cost. Cover can be individually tailored to suit your pet and can be extended to include holiday cancellation, theft, straying and death. Full details are enclosed.

For a free quotation and immediate cover, please ring our Hotline on 0115 254 3383. Alternatively, come along to meet our specially qualified staff at the Norchester Veterinary Centre on Wednesday 24 August between 6 pm and 9 pm. You will find that you can put your mind at rest for a small charge.

Yours sincerely

J Russell
Pet Insurance Manager

Enc

Letters also to: Ms J Christie; Mr L G Mann; and Mrs A M Smith.

Glossary ▶

Action ☞	Keyboard ⌨	Mouse 🖱	Menu 📄
Accents (combination keys)	Select: **International characters** from the **Help** index to see the combinations Hold down/Press keys: As shown *See also*: Symbols		
Alignment of text	*See*: Ragged right margins. Centre text, Justified right margin		
Allocate clear lines	Press: ↵ once for each line required, plus one		
Allocate vertical space			**Format, Paragraphs, Spacing, Before** Key in: The required measurement
AutoCorrect			**Tools, AutoCorrect**
AutoFormat	Press: **Alt + Ctrl + K**		**Format, AutoFormat**
Blocked capitals	Press: **Caps Lock** key		
Bold text	Press: **Ctrl + B**	Click: **B** on the Formatting Tool Bar	**Format, Font**
Borders		Click: ▦ on the Formatting Tool Bar	**Format, Borders and Shading, Borders**
Bulleted lists		Click: ▤ on the Formatting Tool Bar	**Format, Bullets and Numbering Bulleted** Click: On the required style
Capitalise letters	Press: **Ctrl + Shift + A**		**Format, Change Case, Uppercase**
Case of letters (to change)	Press: **Shift + F3**		**Format, Change Case**
Centre text	Press: **Ctrl + E**	Click: ≣ on the Formatting Tool Bar	**Format, Paragraph, Indents and Spacing, Alignment, Centred**
Close a file (clear screen)	Press: **Ctrl + W**		**File, Close**
Copy a block of text Highlight text to be copied	Press: **Ctrl + C**	Click: 📋 on the Standard Tool Bar *or* Press: Right mouse button and Select: **Copy**	**Edit, Copy**
Position cursor where text is to be copied to	Press: **Ctrl + V**	Click: 📋 on the Standard Tool Bar *or* Press: Right mouse button and Select: **Paste**	**Edit, Paste**
Cursor movement Move cursor to required position	Use arrow keys: → ↑ ← ↓	Click: The left mouse button in the required position	
Move to top of document	Press: **Ctrl + Home**		
Move to end of document	Press: **Ctrl + End**		
Move left word by word	Press: **Ctrl + ←**		
Move right word by word	Press: **Ctrl + →**		
Move to end of line	Press: **End**		
Move to start of line	Press: **Home**		
Move to top/bottom of paragraph	Press: **Ctrl + ↑** *or* **Ctrl + ↓**		
Move up/down one screen	Press: **PgUp** *or* **PgDn**		
Cut text	*See*: Delete/cut a block of text		
Date insertion	Press: **Alt + Shift + D**		**Insert, Date and Time**

Action ☞	Keyboard ⌨	Mouse 🖱	Menu 📄
Delete/cut a block of text	Select: Text to be deleted Press: ← (**Del**) *or* Select: Text to be deleted; Press **Ctrl + X**	Select: Text to be deleted/cut: Click: ✂ on the Formatting Tool Bar	Select: Text to be deleted/cut: Select: **Edit**, **Cut** *or* Press: Right mouse button; select: **Cut**
Delete/cut a character	Move cursor to correct character; Press: **Del** *or* Move cursor to right of incorrect character; Press:← (**Del**)		
Delete/cut a word	Select: To end of word Press: ← (**Del**) *or* Select: Word to be deleted: Press: **Ctrl + X**	Select: Word to be deleted/cut: Click: ✂ on the Formatting Tool Bar	Select: Word to be deleted/cut: Select: **Edit**, **Cut** *or* Press: Right mouse button; select: **Cut**
Exit the program	Press: **Alt + F4**	Click: Control button at right of Title Bar	**File**, **Exit**
Enumeration	Key in: The enumeration e.g. A) Press: The **Tab** key Key in: The rest of the text Repeat for each enumerated paragraph	Click: ▤ on the Formatting Tool Bar	**Format**, **Bullets and** **Numbering Numbered** Click: On the required style
Find text	Press: **Ctrl + F**		**File**, **Find**
Font size	Press: **Ctrl + Shift + P** Choose: Desired size	Click: 10 ▾ on the Formatting Tool Bar Choose: Desired size	**Format**, **Font** Choose: Desired size
Next larger point size Next smaller point size	Press: **Ctrl +]** Press: **Ctrl + [**		
Font typeface style	Press: **Ctrl + Shift + F** Choose: Desired font	Click: [Roman] on the Formatting Tool Bar Choose: Desired font	**Format**, **Font** Choose: Desired font
Fractions	*See*: Symbols/Accents/Fractions		
Go to (a specified page)	Press: **Ctrl + G** *or* **F5**		**Edit**, **Go To ...**
Grammar tool	Press: **F7**	Click: ✔ on the Standard Tool Bar	**Tools**, **Spelling and** **Grammar**
Headers and Footers			Select: **View**, **Header and** **Footer** Key in: The header text and/or footer text
To delete:	Select: The actual text or page number Press: ← (**Del**)		
Help function **and Office Assistant**	Press: **F1** (for Contents) Press: **Shift + F1** (for **What's This?** – context- sensitive help)	Click: [?] on the Formatting Tool Bar for the **Office Assistant**	Help
Highlight/shade text		Click: ✏ on the Formatting Tool Bar	**Format**, **Borders and** **Shading**, **Shading**
Indent function Indent at left to next tab stop	Press: **Ctrl + M**	Click: ▤ on the Formatting Tool Bar	**Format**, **Paragraph**, **Indents** **and Spacing**
Indent at left to previous tab stop	Press: **Ctrl + Shift + M**		

Action 🖝	Keyboard ⌨	Mouse 🖱	Menu 📄
Indent as a hanging paragraph	Press: **Ctrl + T**	Click: ⌞▤ on the Formatting Tool Bar	
Unindent and return to standard margin	Press: **Ctrl + Q**		
		Using ruler	
		first-line indent ▽	
		left indent ⌂	
		first-line and left indent ▽⌂	
		right indent △	
Insert special character/symbols	To change the selection to symbol font: Press: **Ctrl + Shift + Q**		To insert a symbol: Position cursor: Where you want the character/symbol to appear: Select: **Insert, Symbol**
Insert text	Simply key in the missing character(s) at the appropriate place – the existing text will 'move over' to make room for the new text. If **OVR** is displayed (overtyping), Press: **Ins(ert)** key to remove		
Italics	Press: **Ctrl + I**	Click: *I* on the Formatting Tool Bar	**Format, Font**
Justified right margin	Press: **Ctrl + J**	Click: ≣ on the Formatting Tool Bar	**Format, Paragraph, Indents and Spacing, Alignment, Justified**
Line break (to insert)	Press: **Shift + ↵**		
Line length – to change	Select text. Display horizontal ruler. Move margin markers to required position on ruler		
Line spacing – to set	Press: **Ctrl + 1** (single) Press: **Ctrl + 2** (double) Press: **Ctrl + 0** (to add or delete a line space)		**Format, Paragraph, Indents and Spacing, Line Spacing**
Mailmerge – add record		**Switch to Data Form** Click: **Add New** Key in: The record Click: **Add New** *or* **Switch to View Source** Click: **Add New** Record Key in: The record	
Mailmerge – amend fields		**Switch to View Source** Click: 🗗 on the Database Tool Bar	
Mailmerge – create data source	Select: **Tools, Mail Merge, Get Data** in Section 2, **Create Data Source**		
Mailmerge – create main document	Select: **Tools, Mail Merge, Create** in Section 1, **Form Letters, Active Window**		
Mailmerge – delete record		Select: **Switch to Data Form** Select: **Find Record** Click: **Delete** *or* Select: **Switch to View Source** Select: The required record Select: **Delete**	
Mailmerge – enter records		**Switch to Data Form** Key in: The record Select: **Add New**	

Action ☞	Keyboard ⌨	Mouse 🖱	Menu 📄
Mailmerge – find record		**Switch to Data Form** Click: **Find** Click: 🖼 Key in: The data Select: **In Field** Click: **Find First** *or* **Switch to Data Form** Click: **View Source**	
Mailmerge – insert merge codes		**Switch to Main Doc** Click: **Insert Merge Field** Select: The required filename	
Mailmerge – open data source		Select: **Tools**, **Mail Merge** Click: **Get Data** in Section 2 Select: **Open Data Source**	
Mailmerge – print merged file		Click: 🖼	
Mailmerge – select records		Select: **Query Options** in the **Mail Merge Helper** dialogue box Select: The required field Key in: The required options	
Mailmerge – sort data source		**Switch to View Source** Place the cursor: In the appropriate column Click: 🖼 or 🖼	
Mailmerge – switch between Data Source and Main Document		Click: 🖼 Select: **Edit** in Section 1 or 2 *OR* Click: 🖼 or 🖼 on the Database Tool Bar	**Window**, **Main Doc** **Window**, **Datafile**
Mailmerge – view merged file		**Switch to Main Doc** Click: 🖼	
Margins (to change)	Use the mouse pointer to drag the left and/or right margin boundaries to the appropriate place on the horizontal ruler. Press: The **Alt** key at the same time 🖼 to view the measurements on screen		**File**, **Page Setup**, **Margins**
Move around document	*See*: Cursor movement		
Move a block of text Select: Text to be moved	Press: **F2** *or* **Ctrl + X**	Click: 🖼 on the Standard Tool Bar	**Edit**, **Cut**
Position cursor where text is to be moved to	Press: **Ctrl + V** *or* ↵	Click: 🖼 on the Standard Tool Bar *drag and drop moving:* Select: Text to be moved Click: Left mouse button in middle of text and keep held down Drag: Selection to required location Release: Mouse button	**Edit**, **Paste** *or* Press: Right mouse button; Select: **Cut** Press: Right mouse button; Select: **Paste**
Open an existing file	Press: **Ctrl + O**	Click: 🖼 on the Standard Tool Bar	**File**, **Open**
Open a new file	Press: **Ctrl + N**	Click: 🖼 on the Standard Tool Bar	**File**, **New**
Page break (to insert)	Press: **Ctrl + ↵**		**Insert**, **Break**, **Page break**
Page numbering	Press: **Alt + Shift + P**		**Insert**, **Page Numbers**
Page Setup			**File**, **Page Setup** Choose from **Margins**, **Paper Size**, **Paper Source** and **Layout**

Action 🖎	Keyboard ⌨	Mouse 🖱	Menu 📄
Paragraphs – splitting/joining	Make a new paragraph (i.e. split a paragraph into two): Move cursor to first letter of new paragraph: Press ↵ twice		
	Join two consecutive paragraphs into one: Move cursor to first letter of new paragraph: Press ← (**Del**) twice (backspace delete key)		
	Press: **Space Bar** (to insert a space after full stop)		
Print out hard copy	Press: **Ctrl + P**	Click: 🖨 on the Standard Tool Bar	**File, Print**
Print Preview	Press: **Ctrl + F2**	Click: 🔍 on the Standard Tool Bar	**File, Print Preview** Select: **Zoom** or **Full Page**
Ragged right margin	Press: **Ctrl + L**	Click: ▤ on the Formatting Tool Bar	**Format, Paragraph, Indents and Spacing, Alignment, Left**
Remove text emphasis First, select the emphasised text to be changed back to normal text	Press: **Ctrl + Space Bar** or Press: **Ctrl + Shift + Z**	Click: Appropriate emphasis button on the Formatting Tool Bar (to deselect)	**Format, Paragraph, Indents and Spacing**
Repeat typing or actions (redo)	Press: **F4** to repeat previous action or Press: **Ctrl + Y**	Click: ↷ on the Formatting Tool Bar To redo (repeat) sets of actions, drag down the **Redo** drop-down list: Select: The group of actions you wish to repeat	**Edit, Repeat Typing**
Replace text	Press: **Ctrl + H**		**Edit, Replace**
Replace text – typeover	1 Select: The incorrect text and then type in the correct entry – Word will fit the replacement text exactly into the original space		
	2 Move cursor: To incorrect entry: Press: The **Ins** key (typeover on) and overtype with correct entry Press: The **Ins** key again (typeover off) to stop overtyping of text		
Restore deleted text	Press: **Ctrl + Z**	Click: ↶ on the Formatting Tool Bar	**Edit, Undo Typing**
Ruler – to display			**View, Ruler**
Save work to disk Save a file for the first time	Press: **F12**		**File, Save As, Enter Filename** Select: Correct Directory/Drive; Click: **OK**
Save an active file which has been saved previously	Press: **Ctrl + S** or Press: **Shift + F12**	Click: 💾 on the Standard Tool Bar	**File, Save**
Save all open files			**File, Save All**
Scroll bars (to view)			**Tools, Options, View** Select: Horizontal Scroll Bar and Vertical Scroll Bar options
Search for text	See Find text		
Select text One character (or more) One word To end of line Start of line A full line A paragraph Whole document Any block of text	Press: **Shift +** → or ← Press: **Shift + Ctrl +** → or ← Press: **Shift + End** Press: **Shift + Home** Press: **Shift + End** or **Home** — Press: **Ctrl + A** —	Click and drag: Pointer across text Double-click: On word Click and drag: Pointer right or down Click and drag: Pointer left or up Click: In selection border Double-click: In selection border Triple-click: In selection border Position pointer: At start of text and Hold down: **Shift**. Then, position pointer at end of text and click	
Remove selection		Click: In any white space	
Sort (rearrange) items			Select: The items or text to be sorted Select: **Table, Sort**
Spaced capitals	Press: **Caps Lock** key. Leave one space after each letter. Leave three spaces after each word		

Action ☞	Keyboard ⌨	Mouse 🖱	Menu 📄
Spellcheck	Press: **F7**	Click: [ABC✓] on the Standard Tool Bar	**Tools, Spelling and Grammar**
Standard Paragraph Files To create/store standard paragraphs: To insert standard paragraphs into your document:	Key in: The portion of text to be saved as a standard paragraph file Save it in a separate file using normal **Save** procedures Position the cursor: Where you want the standard paragaph to be inserted Select: **File** from the **Insert** menu Select/Key in: The appropriate filename		
Status Bar			**Tools, Options, View** Select: Status Bar option
Switch on and load Word		Double-click: **Microsoft Word Icon**	Select: **MS Word from Start**
Symbols	*See*: Inserting special characters/symbols		
Symbols/Accents/Fractions			**Insert, Symbol** Select: The required font Click: On the required symbol Select: **Insert, Close**
Tables Insert table		Click: [▦] on the Standard Tool Bar	**Table, Insert Table**
Tables and borders		Click: [▦] on the Standard Tool Bar	**Table, Draw Table**
Underline text Single underline Double underline	Press: **Ctrl + U** Press: **Ctrl + Shift + W** Press: **Ctrl + Shift + D**	Click: [**U**] on the Formatting Tool Bar	**Format, Font, Underline**
Undo mistakes, typing or actions	Press: **Ctrl + Z**	Click: [↰] on the Standard Tool Bar To undo sets of actions, drag down the **Undo** drop-down list; select: The group of actions you wish to undo	**Edit, Undo Typing**
Units of measurement			**Tools, Options, General, Measurement Units** Select: Desired unit from drop-down menu
View magnified pages		Click: [100%] on the Standard Tool Bar Click: **Magnifies** on Print Preview	**View, Zoom**
View – normal view	Press: **Ctrl + F2**	Click: the [Normal] **Normal View** button at left of document window	**View, Normal**
View – online view		Click: the [Online L] **Online View** button at left of document window	**View, Online**
View – outline view		Click: the [Outline] **Outline View** button at left of document window	**View, Outline**
View – page layout view		Click: the [Page Layout] **Page Layout View** button at left of document window	**View, Page Layout**
View – Print Preview	Press: **Ctrl + F2**	Click: [🔍] on the Standard Tool Bar	**File, Print Preview** Select: **Zoom** or **Full Page**
Widow/orphan control			**Format, Paragraph, Line and Page Breaks**